"Michelle Warren has learned from personal exp....w drawing near to those who hunger for justice can bring us closer to God and God's dream for our lives. *Join the Resistance* is a gift to those who've sensed that the Spirit is stirring in the streets, inviting us to follow Jesus among neighbors crying aloud for their lives. Receive the gift, and join the resistance in Jesus' name."

Jonathan Wilson-Hartgrove, author of *Revolution of Values: Reclaiming Public Faith for the Common Good*

"Recent years have revealed a new generation of women and men who are ready to defy injustice. But how do we move from passion about justice to participation in the day-to-day work for justice? Drawing from the experience of her years of collaborative advocacy and the wisdom of the biblical prophets, Michelle Warren offers us an accessible vision for how each of us—no matter our social location—can join the beautiful resistance."

David Swanson, pastor and author of *Rediscipling the White Church*

"Michelle Warren gets the message of the gospel. She has lived among the oppressed and understands their struggles. In *Join the Resistance* she gives us insight into what is needed to overcome the forces that stop the church from standing for our oppressed sisters and brothers."

Carlos L. Malavé, director of the Latino Christian National Network

"*Join the Resistance* is more than one woman's reflection on her own journey toward racial advocacy. It is testimony to the Spirit's power to transform and use a surrendered life, and a road map for those seeking a way out of supremacist practice into co-conspiracy with God toward the shalom that is only found in justice."

Donna Barber, cofounder and executive director of the Voices Project, author of *Bread for the Resistance: Forty Devotions for Justice People*

"*Join the Resistance* is a call for the people of God to live their beliefs in a way that makes the heart of God tangible in our world. Michelle Warren speaks out of her experience and does so humbly. Her prophetic words do not demand we do more, but they help us see that by joining the resistance we will find the kind of life Jesus came to give, which is 'life to full.'"

Michael Hidalgo, lead pastor of Denver Community Church and host of *The Changing Faith Podcast*

"In *Join the Resistance*, Michelle Warren inspires readers to act at a time when it's most needed. Social justice movements sometimes stall when people don't know what they can do to help. Warren uses her own intriguing personal journey and a collection of historical anecdotes to show how we all have the capability to do extraordinary things. This book is the guide change agents in the making need to go from *can't* to *can*."

Adrian Miller, executive director of the Colorado Council of Churches and author of *Black Smoke*

"*Join the Resistance* describes resistance to the powers and principalities as the work of one community—a community made up of biblical prophets, activists throughout history, and faithful advocates today. It will convict you of your apathy and inspire you with biblical teaching. But most importantly, it will equip you with resources for joining that community's work in the world today. This book is not merely about Michelle's journey, it is about how to live a life upended by the coming kingdom of God and shaped by the faithful work of the family of God."

Kaitlyn Schiess, author of *The Liturgy of Politics*

"Michelle Warren knows of what she writes. This book is rich in Bible-based theology, but even richer in real-life, concrete practice based in Michelle's lived experience. Her humility and self-awareness show in her admission she doesn't know it all and still has much to learn about injustice. Still, she doesn't use ignorance to excuse inaction. Instead, Michelle takes what Dietrich Bonhoeffer called the risky venture of responsible action, concerned more for the well-being of those who suffer in the margins than for her doing that action perfectly. You won't know everything after reading *Join the Resistance*, but you will know enough to step out in faith and help others pursue God's justice while deepening your understanding of it. This book is a gift to all who need justice and those who desire to help them find it."

Rob Schenck, president of the Dietrich Bonhoeffer Institute, Washington, DC, and author of *Costly Grace: An Evangelical Minister's Rediscovery of Faith, Hope, and Love*

"Weaving personal narrative with the witness of ancient prophets and modern-day saints, Warren forges a pathway toward our collective resistance and liberation."

Michael-Ray Mathews, deputy director of Faith in Action and host of the *Prophetic Resistance Podcast*

"Michelle has truly done a marvelous work in this book. Michelle speaks from such a captivating lens because she joined the resistance many years ago and is now writing about what she knows, not just what she heard or read. In this book, Michelle makes the assertion, 'There is a huge divide along racial, political, and theological lines. In today's cancel culture we are led to believe that people are too far gone for us to even attempt to build bridges.' Michelle then goes on to tell us in plain and simple terms how to build those bridges. I've been privileged to work with Michelle for several years in the good work of kingdom justice, and she is one of the best bridge builders I know. I hope this book blesses you as much as it has me. From time to time I get weary in this work, and Michelle has reignited a flame of hope in me to continue to walk toward freedom and share liberation."
Daniel Henley, chief spiritual officer of Agape Child and Family Services and pastor of Journey Church, Memphis

"In *Join the Resistance*, Michelle Warren lifts up the biblical narrative alongside the stories of modern freedom fighters. She leans in to her own substantial experience to offer practical wisdom for those wanting to join the long, faithful struggle for justice. Her advice is humble and thoughtful. She inspires courage and rightfully centers the voices and stories of those impacted by injustice rather than those wanting to help. In these pages, those new to the work will find expert guidance while experienced advocates will be encouraged and reminded of why they joined the resistance in the first place."
Stephen K. Reeves, director of advocacy with Cooperative Baptist Fellowship and executive director of Fellowship Southwest

"This is a book for our time! Exposure of the church's complicity with injustice, though long overdue, has been a marked and painful characteristic in recent years. Warren's clarion call to join the resistance overflows from decades of deep faith, unwavering rootedness in the margins, and commitment to the pursuit of justice. She brilliantly weaves personal narrative and lessons from the biblical prophets together with powerful music lyrics to create a compelling guidebook and soundtrack for justice seeking. As inspiring as it is practical, this book will move you. Read it and join the resistance!"
Lisa Rodriguez-Watson, national director, Missio Alliance

"*Join the Resistance* is a worthwhile and meaningful read for any justice seeker. Not only does Michelle have an intellectual command of this topic, even more so, she lives it out in her daily life."
Robert Gelinas, author and lead pastor of Colorado Community Church

"I am grateful for Michelle Warren's wisdom and witness in *Join the Resistance*. Warren deftly tells her own story while keeping the stories of marginalized people at the center. For privileged Christians like me who are seeking ways to advocate for justice in the public square, this book is a guide, an exhortation, and a call to courage and humility."

Amy Julia Becker, author of *To Be Made Well* and *White Picket Fences*

"This book is an excellent starting point for people who are looking to become more deeply involved in resistance work in their communities. Warren lays out compelling stories from Scripture, her own life, and the lives of other movement leaders to show how important it is for every Christian and every person to 'come to the table' and join this work. *Join the Resistance* offers a prophetic call with concrete action steps for people who are new to movement work, as well as sustaining wisdom and encouragement for those of us who are committed to the long haul."

Jennifer Butler, founder in residence of Faith in Public Life

"In *Join the Resistance*, Michelle Warren shares hard-earned wisdom for those of us who desire to see change and overcome evil with good. Warren forthrightly acknowledges the wisdom she shares is communal—often originating with the most marginalized people in US history. Indeed, this book is most powerful because Michelle humbly practices what she preaches. I have observed her life and have read this book, and they are both true. She is among the wisest people I know. Even so, she shares insight that is not always easy to swallow, but necessary if we are to be righteous, which entails being just. Is it possible to have so much good judgment stashed in one place? It must be—because it is right here. I cannot recommend this book highly enough for those of us who seek to act like Jesus in a polarized society where the church is often complicit in wrongdoing."

Marlena Graves, author of *The Way Up is Down*

"Michelle's book is exactly what any advocate needs to understand the most profound insights and most basic practices of justice work. I've known Michelle for over ten years and worked with her in the movement, and this book makes you feel like you are having a one-on-one conversation with her. She invites you to consider uncomfortable truths and journey into learned experiences from years of relentless commitment to bravery, love, and selflessness."

Agustin Quiles, founding president and CEO of Mission Talk

"In *Join the Resistance*, Michelle Warren expertly weaves together Scripture, theology, and personal experience to inspire and challenge all of us to embrace the intersectional activism that our faith requires. This book is a timely, compelling, and provocative read, equipping and mobilizing all of us to become better allies in the struggle for a radically more just and inclusive United States."

Adam Taylor, president of Sojourners and author of *A More Perfect Union: A New Vision for Building the Beloved Community*

"Michelle Warren reminds us all that faith is not just about what we believe. It is about how those beliefs move us to take action. Scripture itself says that we can have faith to move mountains, but if we don't have love it is meaningless. Following Jesus is a call to live out the revolutionary, countercultural values of the upside-down kingdom of God, where the last are first and the first are last, where the mighty are cast down from their thrones and the lowly are lifted up. This book is an invitation into that revolution."

Shane Claiborne, author of *The Irresistible Revolution* and cofounder of Red Letter Christians

"Michelle Warren believes that the God of the Bible is not just one of charity, but the God of justice. She shows why social action is only the beginning and must lead to public advocacy to make structural change that alleviates oppression. Her amazing personal story of becoming an activist is on wonderful display here as she tells so many other compelling stories of people who are changing things. Michelle has learned the important lesson that just 'showing up' is not enough, but 'how you show up' is now crucial. This book is a teaching tool, especially for white privileged activists like Michelle, who can learn how to show up well. I think the prophet Amos would smile over this book and exclaim, 'Let justice roll.'"

Jim Wallis, chair in faith and justice and director of the Center on Faith and Justice at Georgetown University, author of *America's Original Sin*

"In *Join the Resistance*, Michelle Warren teaches us how to serve the movement, stay at the table, and help our people. However, she does not do this through lecture and conjecture but through engaging narrative, challenging reframing, and relational humility. I am thankful for her lifelong witness and her desire to push so that none of us sit on the sidelines but step into the good work of kingdom justice."

Jonathan Brooks, pastor and author of *Church Forsaken*

Silvia R. Jordan

FOREWORD BY LATASHA MORRISON

MICHELLE FERRIGNO WARREN

JOIN THE RESISTANCE

STEP INTO THE
GOOD WORK OF
KINGDOM
JUSTICE

AFTERWORD BY DOMINIQUE DuBOIS GILLIARD

An imprint of InterVarsity Press
Downers Grove, Illinois

InterVarsity Press
P.O. Box 1400 | Downers Grove, IL 60515-1426
ivpress.com | email@ivpress.com

InterVarsity Press® is the publishing division of InterVarsity Christian Fellowship/USA®. For more information, visit intervarsity.org.

All Scripture quotations, unless otherwise indicated, are taken from The Holy Bible, New International Version®, NIV®. Copyright © 1973, 1978, 1984, 2011 by Biblica, Inc.™ Used by permission of Zondervan. All rights reserved worldwide. www.zondervan.com. The "NIV" and "New International Version" are trademarks registered in the United States Patent and Trademark Office by Biblica, Inc.™

While any stories in this book are true, some names and identifying information may have been changed to protect the privacy of individuals.

Tree illustration by Silvia R. Jordan, 2022. Used by permission.

The publisher cannot verify the accuracy or functionality of website URLs used in this book beyond the date of publication.

Cover design and image composite: David Fassett
Interior design: Daniel van Loon

ISBN 978-1-5140-0433-3 (print) | ISBN 978-1-5140-0434-0 (digital)

Printed in the United States of America ∞

Library of Congress Cataloging-in-Publication Data
A catalog record for this book is available from the Library of Congress.

29   28   27   26   25   24   23   22 | 8   7   6   5   4   3   2   1

TO BARBARA, KIT, ALEXIA, AND MARY,

for steadying your shoulders and lighting the way so others coming
behind you could stand and continue to build
on the good work of kingdom justice.

CONTENTS

FOREWORD

LATASHA MORRISON

I FIRST MET MICHELLE IN CHICAGO in July 2016. We were at a gathering for Christian justice leaders from around the United States at a time when the country and the church were becoming deeply divided along racial and political lines. Michelle and I were new to this group but not new to the conversation.

As we sat side by side in a discussion group, Michelle asked me about myself. I stated candidly, "I am a pastor at a White megachurch in Texas." Michelle's eyes widened and her face fell. She slowly and quietly responded. "Wow. I'm sorry" was all she said.

As a White woman who for decades had lived, worked, and worshiped in majority BIPOC communities, Michelle understood the unique challenges working across racial lines, especially for me as a Black woman pastor serving a White congregation in Texas. For a season, she had lived in Dallas teaching middle school in a poor community of color and had experienced the racial and political tensions that existed in Texas. We did not say much as we sat there; the few words stated said enough.

We exchanged contact information and went on to intersect over the next several years in various spaces but always from that shared space of seeing each other as bridge builders.

I did not stay at that Texas church much longer. In 2016 I founded Be the Bridge, which seeks to "empower people and culture toward racial healing, equity, and reconciliation." In my ongoing work and book *Be the Bridge*, I talk about the steps needed to move beyond awareness to the restorative work of making reconciliation a lifestyle.

We cannot fix what we don't understand. So we seek to understand the social and political construct of race and how to move toward racial solidarity and holistic restoration. You don't have to do it all, of course. But you can identify racial wrongs in the world around you and take one step toward making them right. That's the work of reparations. That's the work of the gospel.

Jesus came to restore individual people and break down systems of oppression, to provide a way for his kingdom to appear on earth as it is in heaven. He came so that we his followers could partner with him in restoring integrity and justice to broken systems, broken governments, and ultimately broken relationships. By building a bridge between the oppressed and the oppressors, he created space at the table and opened the conversation to explore a new way forward to build a future together.

To do this important restorative gospel work, we need to learn from others. Those who have been stepping into the troubled waters to resist racial injustice and division with the light of Christ can help us all know where to go.

Michelle is one of those light-shining kinds of people. She has been stepping into good work that actively repairs and restores what is broken at every level, from individual restoration and social justice transformation to the work of dismantling systemic injustice.

She helps shine this light on a new, necessary way forward in this book. She does not leave people with an imperative to go and do without showing us a way. As she says—how you show up is as important as showing up. From the Prophets and Jesus' parables to those who have gone before us, Michelle guides us forward, helping us set a new trajectory to restore racial brokenness through faith-rooted activism.

Many of us hide little flickers of hope inside our hearts, and we ignore the small nudges from God pushing us to change the direction of our lives. When we don't follow his leadings, we end up carrying on in the status quo even if it's not the right thing, the most just thing. We have to be willing to shake things up, even if stepping into our calling leads us into deep pain and discomfort.

As you read the following principles for a life of love rooted in action and truth, please don't sleep on it. Move, act, and get involved in the good work of kingdom justice by resisting the status quo and seeking restorative justice together. Bridges are built not with passivity or avoidance but with the deep, hard work of seeking to understand—the deep hard work of fighting for justice for all.

INTRODUCTION

How to Step into the Good Work

INJUSTICE DOES NOT JUST HAPPEN, and it does not repair itself.

A while back, I joined a virtual book club with people who were reading my first book, *The Power of Proximity*. After talking, sharing, and answering questions, one of the participants asked if I thought the *only* way to heal injustice was through direct advocacy.

I answered no yet went on to share why I believe activism—which includes advocacy, or taking your convictions to the public square—is an essential key toward overcoming injustice.

From the beginning of time, when everything that was good and perfect became broken and put evil on full display, we have been warring with our fellow humans. Those struggles and wars center around power—who has it and who needs it? Power not only has guaranteed seats at the table, but it also has voice and access to get what it needs and wants. Those held down by injustice cannot even consider the power table as they struggle to manage one more day completely dependent on the systems that keep them in their place.

Those systems that work for some are keeping others in perpetual brokenness. This is not okay. For those of us who call ourselves Christians, who believe that in the reconciling work of Christ and his gospel we are to no longer operate in this post-fall, pre-Pentecost narrative, there is no difference between Jew or Greek (racial/cultural), slave or free (socioeconomic), male or female (gender); we are all one in Christ. If we share this oneness, then we must submit to and work together toward ensuring that everyone is treated with dignity and respect. This is not happening as it should. We must be willing, as a foundational practice of our faith, to stand against oppressive, unjust systems by confronting power.

Confrontation of power is not new. From the early days of the prophets who confronted leaders accused of the very same injustices our leaders are today, to Jesus who stood tall against the rulers of his day, calling out their disregard for the marginalized and use of power to perpetuate fear, the Bible clearly shows us just how important and familiar this practice of faith is.

Today, people are working to build power in the streets and confront formal power to make change, whether we are aware of them or not. They are shaping and sharing the much-needed message for change. We need to care enough to listen to them and to join them. For over two decades I have been joining up alongside community leaders—attending meetings, marching, praying, singing, whatever we needed to do to get a little farther down the line for justice. I have seen change. I have seen some wins. I have shared many losses. Every day we get back up, shake ourselves off, and begin again.

Recently I have seen new faces show up, many of them White and many of them privileged. They are waking up to a new awareness and the need for systemic change. They, too, are discontent with the status quo and want to build a better world now and for future generations. This is great because the movement needs them, especially those with access to power.

As a White, privileged, long-standing justice advocate and activist, it's important for me to share this: *how you show up is just as important as showing up*. I cannot implore you enough to learn your place in this moment, your moment in history and in the long-standing movement toward justice and healing. Hence, the reason for this book.

Over the years, through directly impacted neighbors, friends, and mentors, I have learned a lot about how to walk in, how to serve the movement, how to stay at the table, and how to help my people. I am still growing. I have made and continue to make mistakes; I try to learn from them. I also have some things to share; I want others like me, who care deeply about pain and injustice and hold the belief that we are not victims to the status quo, to understand how to show up and effectively work toward the collective good.

I must include this important disclaimer—I am a faith-rooted activist. I join alongside good work that is happening for the betterment of my community. Though I participate in activism as an expression of my Christian faith, not all activists are rooted in that same faith; but that does not mean what they are working toward isn't faith-filled. Not all actions I join are led by churches or people from churches, but that doesn't mean God is not in the center of it or isn't using it for good. Whether the efforts are defined as secular or sacred, I am walking in with conviction, joining Christ in his restorative gospel.

Throughout this book I highlight stories of activists who picked up the work of righting the wrongs of injustice in history. I believe that in joining the resistance and serving the movement, we need to also become students of the resistance. We need to learn whose shoulders we stand on and continue to build on their foundational work. Songs and poems are powerful words of hope, boldly expressed in art that inspires and helps drive the work of resistance. I have ended each chapter with a song or poem that has shaped resistance work, and there are others sprinkled throughout.

The voices and work of resistance are demonstrated over and over in Scripture, most clearly through the voices of the prophets. So, I also highlight prophets' messages, as well as the parables of the prophet Jesus, who was God himself come to earth to redeem, reconcile, and demonstrate for us a better way forward.

My hope is that this book will help ignite a remnant of people to show up in the streets in the moment and learn how to become connected, not only for one day but for the whole movement of justice. Friends, this is the work—the good, important work that moves us beyond words toward bold action grounded in truth (1 John 3:18).

Join up and take your place in the work of resistance where the first become last and the last become first, where the voices closest to the pain lead us, until justice flows down the river with ease, and righteousness is a nonstop, life-giving stream.

PART I

SERVE THE MOVEMENT

1

WALKING IN

MONDAY, MAY 25, STARTED LIKE ANY OTHER Monday beginning a week, and my youngest was days away from graduating from high school. I was so excited to celebrate with him and all he had accomplished, especially his final semester that had been interrupted by the Covid-19 pandemic closing schools and moving students to online learning.

At the time I was serving as Advocacy and Strategic Engagement Director for Christian Community Development Association and I was supporting our newly hired president, an African American pastor from Minneapolis, Minnesota. With only three weeks under her belt, much of our time at work was spent helping her understand the details of our shared work. It wasn't supposed to be a heavy pressure time. We were adjusting daily to the pandemic inconveniences, but we were taking it in stride. It was a gentle beginning—or so we thought.

Over the course of the next couple of days, a video of a Black man being murdered by a White police officer began to go viral. The Black man was George Floyd, a name that would be heard around the globe, impressing on people from communities across the world to march in the streets, calling for justice, chanting Black lives mattered, and renewing conviction that we needed to stop senseless, racially driven murders.

Because my work was in the advocacy space, my days those weeks were emotional and long, listening, connecting, and concerting with our community leaders, supporting them in their grief and response. My new boss who lived in Minneapolis shared her daily perspective of her city that was literally burning. The grief was palpable and desperate.

Rioting and looting had not only been happening in Minneapolis where George Floyd's murder took place, but also in cities across the country. The anger and frustration spilling from the Black community had reached a fevered pitch and they were demanding change. The pandemic kept us all a little closer to home than during the days of Mike Brown and the Ferguson protests, yet in my city of Denver the response looked similar. Marching, protests, and counterprotests drew harsh criticism, sparking division. Peaceful protests at times became riotous. The status quo was being shaken up.

Between the graduation celebrations and long work hours supporting leaders in cities across the country, it took me several days to join the marches. When I did go, my son Wil and his friend joined me, both new high school graduates of Denver Public Schools (DPS). DPS was leading the effort that day, centering Black students. High school students like my son's friend were invited to join the front of the parade, riding in the flatbed truck that was directing the marchers.

As we walked together, chanting familiar refrains, I felt so grateful for my city, its leaders, and my three kids, all DPS graduates. We all had marched for many years alongside our neighborhood friends for fair immigration laws, against racialized policing, and against other issues that continued to perpetuate brokenness in our community. Even amid such hard things, it was an important time of community and solidarity. I was so glad I was able to share it with people from all over my city and Colorado.

While there was a familiarity as we hit the streets to show solidarity and call for change, this time was unlike anything I had experienced before. First, there were thousands and thousands of people pouring onto the streets to walk down Colfax toward the Martin Luther King Jr. statue in Denver's City Park. I couldn't recall a march that had drawn so many people. Second, many were young families with kids and strollers in tow. Third, so many were White; I had never seen so many White people come out in support of justice for people of color.

I should not have been surprised because I had been hearing the same thing from friends around the country and had seen it in pictures on social media, but now I was sharing the experience at my city's march. White people were out in droves. They wore Black Lives Matter T-shirts, something I was criticized for by the White community just a few years before. This was a different moment. I was skeptical but mostly I was really encouraged. Maybe a tide was turning? Maybe this was no longer a Black or Brown thing, but it was a community thing?

It was a good day, but it was far from unicorns and rainbows. As the blocks got longer and the loudspeaker became harder to hear, it didn't take long to see some bad practices. What I observed was that the White people didn't know how to protest. They didn't know how to chant, follow well, or keep the energy going. There were a few of us working on following the front but it didn't take long to see people begin to move forward to be better connected with the front of the action.

Seasoned marchers know not to show up with our own agenda, but rather to follow the leader, repeat their message, posture our actions after theirs. In this case it was Black men. A Black man had been murdered; Black men are the most at-risk to be shot and killed by police than any other people group. Following them were Black women, children, and young people.

As Wil and I marched we would see Black people come behind and we would take an instinctive step back, affording them space to pass. We understand that when marching, you center and follow people closest to the pain. That day this learned practice was not understood by many others. You could tell this was a new experience for those who had not had a lifestyle of community solidarity and marching.

Strollers don't push easily toward the front, so many White families stayed toward the back of the line, but over time I saw young White teenagers and several White men begin to work their way forward. Then, what started as moving forward became pushing. I couldn't believe what I was seeing—White people pushing Black people aside so they could get a better view!

As I looked out on this crowd of new protesters, who I believe in their hearts wanted to join the collective chorus, all I could think was, *My people. Oh, my people. We don't even know how to walk right.* Didn't they know that it wasn't about them? That it wasn't about them getting a good view? Didn't they know that they were there to join and add their voices, not to push them to the front?

That's when I realized, they didn't. No one had taught them to understand their place in this moment. No one had taught them that the moment did not start with their awareness and response that day. It was a good thing to wake up and respond to the current pain and injustice, but they did not realize they were joining in and following a long-standing current for justice.

They did not realize efforts like these had been going on for years and generations before, whose efforts were not about one person or one issue, one video or one march, but an ongoing movement of resistance and solidarity, until everyone has justice. Their marching that day was just a beginning and like everyone else, they needed to learn their place in the moment and the bigger, overall work of resisting injustice.

LEARNING YOUR PLACE

I had just wrapped up a conference in Memphis, Tennessee, and I joined fellow colleagues to tour the Civil Rights Museum at the Lorraine Motel. The Lorraine Motel is where Martin Luther King Jr. was shot and killed. After that dreadful day, the owner of the motel, Walter Bailey, memorialized Room 306, King's room, by keeping it untouched and unrented. After the motel's permanent closure in 1988, the building was purchased and opened as a museum in 1991.[1]

The museum tells the story of civil rights for African Americans from the early days of the slave trade until the present—it's an important memorial to the story and collective work of racial justice. Though I remember much of the museum and its informational and emotional journey, one of the more poignant moments was inside a replica of a Montgomery city bus with a life-sized sculpture of Rosa Parks sitting at the front. I walked through the bus with one of my colleagues and her elementary-aged daughter. I paused by Rosa Parks's sculpture and saw a depiction of her small frame and resolute face. My heart filled with deep admiration and gratitude for her bravery and leadership in the resistance work needed to promote civil rights.

Before I got off the bus, I looked back at my friend. She too stopped by the sculpture, then bent down and quietly spoke to her daughter. To this day I recall the image vividly. My friend, a Black woman from Chicago, later told me she wanted her daughter to understand all that those strong Black women and men had done to afford them the opportunities they had. She shared how important it was to walk the museum together.

Several years later I went back to the museum with another group of colleagues. This time I boarded the bus behind two of the African American women in our group. I stood in the back of the bus waiting as I watched each woman walk from back to front and place their hand on Rosa Parks's shoulder, audibly thanking her for all that she did for them and for Black people. I felt so grateful to share what I considered a sacred moment as well as a literal reminder of my place in the work.

However, inspired by Rosa Parks I may be, hers is not my story, nor the story of people who look like me. My shared efforts of racial solidarity and resistance to the status quo, while necessary and important, are not the same. I am there to follow the leadership and join the work; I am there to serve the movement.

FIRST STEPS

When my oldest child was in first grade, I received a call from a school parent asking for some support. This was not unusual, as the school had recently been built on community-driven support and was now in its second year. For several years' prior, community leaders had worked with the school board, with mill-levy bonds for funding, and with thousands of community participants to open the very first dual-language public Montessori school in the country.

It was exciting to join in support of this revolutionary new school that intentionally prioritized the value of equity and global citizenship. Half of the student body were native Spanish speakers, half native English—all learning together in two languages. Working across racial and cultural lines on behalf of this outstanding prototype was electric. It seemed like everyone associated with the school was a nonprofit leader, artist, teacher, or activist.

The second year the school was operating, a ballot amendment for the State of Colorado was to be brought to a vote. If it passed, English would be the only language students who did not speak English would be able to be taught. Our hard-fought, dual-language school model would tank. Cries from our community rose immediately and the need to organize, protest, call, resist was put into full swing.

When a parent called me to help get the news out, the request was simple—would you please make sure each parent in my child's class got a flier when they picked their student up? Of course! It was the least I could do. I put a copy of each flier in every student's box. Easy. Job done.

Later that afternoon I got a call from the principal—you can't put political material in school boxes. Oh, well. I apologized and picked up my fliers at the school office. I began again, this time doing whatever I could to physically get the flier in each parent's hand.

No one was asking me to do anything else. I chose to join the march that weekend, put signs on my car, talk to everyone I knew about the horrible amendment, but in the actual organizing work, I was only asked to hand out fliers. That was good. I was new to activism and protest work—I hadn't even realized the extent of what was happening.

Later that month, when I piled my young kids into the family car and joined the protest march, I had never yet been a part of a protest march; I had never been on the front page of a newspaper; I had never chanted—this was my walking in. I did what I was asked. I brought my voice and my body, and alongside my neighborhood I shouted, "No on *treinta y uno*. No on thirty-one." I was simply there to serve, to follow, to join.

JOINING UP

Joining our school community that season, I had no idea it would be a beginning of a life defined by activism. I had been heavily involved in nonprofit community development work but taking my personal convictions to a public place by marching was new.

The decade prior I had been a seventh-grade math teacher who worked in schools that state standards had declared failing. Nearly all my students came from families from a nearby housing project. They struggled with physical safety, educational opportunities, housing, and food security, among other things. After that season of teaching, I moved back to my home state of Colorado and, alongside my husband, David, started a home for homeless teenage girls.

I was deeply grateful to be able to move from a classroom where I interacted with students less than one hour a day to living alongside teen girls as they made brave, important choices to move their lives forward. After we started the transitional house, we worked alongside our church to form Open Door Ministries, a community development corporation that would provide the structure for the house we started and other existing and future social justice ministry programming for our church's community.

My life was daily being shaped by social concerns stemming from poverty, racism, and immigration. Addressing those concerns in and with the community allowed in me the growth of deep roots of compassion and conviction to work toward change. It didn't take long for me to begin to understand that though the value of individual restoration and social justice was paramount, unless systems changed, we would never see the racial healing and community transformation we all desperately longed for and needed.

By the time I was asked to join in the school's fight against a bad amendment by handing out fliers and marching, I had already been serving on the front lines of social justice work, experiencing systemic barriers that would not simply right themselves. I was growing in my understanding that loving my neighbors and neighborhood also included my willingness to join them and confront systems of injustice.

CONFRONTING SYSTEMS

Injustice is not okay. In recent years, people have been waking up, some for the first time, to the reality that systems do not work for everyone, that elections are important, and that leadership is needed to unite a divided people. This awareness, while deeply grievous, is good, because joining the good work necessary to change systems requires people.

As a Christian, I am driven by my love for Christ and his love for others. My rootedness to the teachings of the Bible and the importance of living out what it says is central to my identity. It is both my faith and my practice. I also grew up in the church, and in addition to my spiritual formation, I was terrific at Sunday school. Being a good Sunday school kid not only meant you knew your way around the Bible, but you also caught and practiced all the added on, cultural expectations of the church. I was trained to love God, love others, and be a good Pharisee.

I knew what behaviors and attitudes were and were not acceptable in the church. I was not only good at knowing the rules, but I excelled at following them. I share this because I knew then as much as I know now that mixing politics and the church is a big no-no. You could be a little political by identifying with one political party and working to reverse *Roe v. Wade* and gay marriage, but any other political thought or idea could lead to becoming the community pariah.

I gave no thought to that cultural rule before I became a teacher, before I moved into a community impacted by poverty, racism, and immigration status, before political issues and elected power made a difference in the health and wellness of my community. Before all that, the system worked for me and those I loved. After, the system still worked for me, but I could see how it was perpetuating hardship with little way out for my church community, neighbors, and friends. I could not deny that reality. Change needed to happen.

As I started to share what I was seeing and to tell the truth of all I was learning, I was getting closer and closer to that forbidden line—don't mix politics with the church. You can love the poor by meeting their immediate needs (mercy), you can even look more deeply into the problems and provide a social or community development response (social justice), but do not get political. Do not speak against the systems that keep the status quo in play. Do not cross that forbidden road.

It was much like the journey of the Samaritan along the Jericho Road, who crossed over to help minister to the half-dead, beaten man, but after several years of helping hurting people I realized it's not okay to have a road that perpetuates the beating, robbing, and potential death of its travelers.[2]

If I was going to follow God's greatest commandment to love him with all my heart, all my soul, all my strength, and all my mind, as well as love my neighbor as myself, it was not okay if my family and I were good, and my neighbor wasn't. I realized that bold, radical love was not simply crossing a forbidden line but working to remove it entirely so that nothing stood in the way of working toward justice.

FAITH-ROOTED ACTIVISM

Somewhere in the journey of loving my neighbors, I had become an activist. Initial steps into that label honestly seemed foreign and a little uncomfortable. Having not known any activists in my early formation made it seem far off—the term connoted images of people that seemed extreme. I had moved, however, from silent observer of my community's stories to fellow steward. Stewarding means you assume or take some responsibility, ensuring that something gets done about a situation.

Taking some responsibility did not mean I was taking over; ensuring something got done didn't mean doing it my way. It simply meant that I needed to decide: Was I in the work or outside of it? Was I sharing and responding appropriately to the pain alongside my community or simply making notes about it and relaying it as a commentator?

I chose to be all in.

Not everyone is going to make choices like I did—that is not the point. The point is, as Christians who care about social justice, moving from the sidelines to join the sacred work of faith-rooted activism needs to be intentional. However long your season to steward is, it needs to be stewarded well. It is not enough to simply become dissatisfied and commentate on the status quo. We must move toward substantive, restorative action that moves against the current of conformity, demanding a better, more just way.

The gospel, or good news, of Christ is a restorative work. At its center is God's heart for justice. God's justice, satisfied through Christ's salvific work, gives humanity a way back to God. The liberating power of the gospel puts us in right relationship with God, and as agents of his salt and light in the world, he invites us to join him in reconciling all things to himself. This restoration of *all* things goes well beyond the spiritual and encompasses a commitment to holistic restoration including emotional, mental, and physical restoration. This is the good, restorative work that we are called to join Christ in doing.

Jesus came to earth to shake things up, to introduce a new way forward, to usher in the kingdom of God. At the beginning of his earthly ministry, he went to the synagogue in Nazareth where he grew up. He stood up and read a prophecy from Isaiah that described his purpose in the world: "The Spirit of the Lord is on me, because he has anointed me to proclaim good news to the poor. He has sent me to proclaim freedom for the prisoners and recovery of sight for the blind, to set the oppressed free" (Luke 4:18). He then said, "Today this scripture is fulfilled in your hearing" (Luke 4:21).

Jesus came with purpose, to proclaim good news and freedom for the most oppressed in society. He came to heal some from physical blindness, and to reveal himself and his truth to people who were and remain blinded by lies and darkness. His reconciliation work of salvation was the starting point.

His radical message of a new kingdom defied power, religious practices, and superiority. Evidenced in humbly coming to earth, he demonstrated for us a new way forward, weaving together the justice of God with the sacrificial love of Christ. We see in 1 John 3:18 that it is not enough to simply love in words and speech, but we must also love *with actions* and *in truth*.

Being able to see pain, brokenness, injustice, and oppression is a grace; to tell its truth is transformative. Once we see the truth, we can accept our commission to join Jesus in his ongoing redemptive, restorative work. This restorative kingdom justice work gives birth to and compels us toward honest action that resists oppression and injustice at every level, especially the oppression of the vulnerable.

Faith-rooted activism allows our commitment of love to be on full display. This long, restorative, justice work is the long work of the kingdom. Whether it is the justice of God toward individual, social, or structural entities, we join with Christ in his redemptive work of restoration, not just in *word*. Our living, public witness to the wholeness of God's restoration is the good, necessary work of the people of God. Honest action that is founded on the justice of God, demonstrated in the love of Christ, and practiced by the people of God compels us to not stay silent in the face of injustice but instead to speak boldly against oppression.

A NEW KINGDOM, A NEW WAY

When Jesus started his ministry on earth, he came with a new, unfamiliar message—there was no more waiting for the Messiah; he had come. A new kingdom was being ushered in and there was no time to look back, the kingdom was here. But his forward-facing, new kingdom message, filled with prophetic conviction and holy fire, was met with resistance by the leaders of the day.

Jesus was a friend of sinners, a man acquainted with grief. He was a miracle doer, a feeder of thousands, a forgiver of sins, and a teacher. His teachings were new, yet familiar. The common people of the day were able to hear and follow him—God seemed close, and indeed he was! Jesus was God formed in man and fully present in their midst. Jesus' love for the marginalized, the poor, the vulnerable was radical.

Centering a message that was good news to the marginalized infuriated the Jewish leaders of the day and drove them to plot to and eventually kill Jesus. Those leaders wanted to continue to center themselves and keep the poor from ever attaining the love, liberation, and redemption of God.

Shortly into Jesus' ministry, he pulled together a group of disciples. Disciples were not a unique thing at that time. Pharisees had disciples; John the Baptist had disciples. But Jesus' disciples were different. Jesus' ragtag group of men and their unrefined ways of doing things drew harsh criticism from the leaders of the day. The Pharisees did not miss an opportunity to challenge both Jesus and the actions of his disciples.

One day this distinction of disciples and the practice of fasting came up. John the Baptist and the Pharisee's disciples fasted, but Jesus' were going around eating and drinking, and with the "wrong kind" of people. Jesus was asked about this, and he taught through a parable:

> No one tears a piece out of a new garment to patch an old one. Otherwise, they will have torn the new garment, and the patch from the new will not match the old. And no one pours new wine into old wineskins. Otherwise, the new wine will burst the skins; the wine will run out and the

wineskins will be ruined. No, new wine must be poured into new wineskins. And no one after drinking old wine wants the new, for they say, "The old is better." (Luke 5:36-39)

Jesus began to share this message about the new work God was doing through him and continues to do today—new practices, new messengers. God would use new ways to steward his never-changing truth in the world. In time new wine in new wineskins would yield good results that satisfy. One cannot get great old wine taste without being willing to use new wine and new wineskins.

Winemaking is not simply about which skins you pour into. It is a long, process-driven work. After you plant, nurture, and harvest the grapes, you must wash, crush, and strain the juice before putting it in the wineskins to ferment and become aged. Would you really want to do all that work and put it in a familiar, old, or used wineskin that is going to burst? What a futile effort! It's the entire process that makes a wine great, not just the wineskin. New ways of holding something of value and allowing them to become seasoned can be a good thing.

Don't allow yourself to become so nostalgic, rigid, or judgmental about the way God chooses to demonstrate his message that you miss a new way forward. God is always bringing forth his message and heart in new methods. Can we be open and ask him to help us see how he is restoring and making things new? Can we see him doing new things? Can we perceive it?

CAN WE PERCEIVE IT?

The prophet Isaiah, another forward-thinking truth teller, lived about seven hundred years before the birth of Christ. Isaiah was the prophet that told Judah they were going to be captured because they were so sinful and had walked away from God. He also spoke about the coming of Christ and his redemptive work that would ultimately bring the people back to God.

In Isaiah 43 we see Isaiah speak to Judah's impending captivity. Up north, Israel had already been captured by the Assyrians for the same behaviors and practices that Judah was also doing: worshiping other gods, not caring for the poor, and centering personal gain regardless of God's law. God's justice and righteousness were being disregarded and captivity was in their future also.

Despite this impending reality, God's message to his people in Isaiah 43 is one of encouragement and reminder:

> Do not fear, for I have redeemed you; I have summoned you by name; you are mine. When you pass through the waters, I will be with you; and when you pass through the rivers, they will not sweep over you. When you walk through the fire, you will not be burned; the flames will not set you ablaze. For I am the LORD your God, the Holy One of Israel, your Savior. (vv. 1-3)

No matter how terrible things looked. No matter how abandoned they felt, God would never leave them. He had chosen them and would not ultimately destroy them, and in time would bring them back together.

> I will bring your children from the east and gather you from the west. I will say to the north, "Give them up!" and to the south, "Do not hold them back." Bring my sons from afar and my daughters from the ends of the earth—everyone who is called by my name, whom I created for my glory, whom I formed and made. (vv. 5-7)

God was unlike any other gods. He had shown himself powerful and faithful before and would do it again. Redemption, the nature of God, would rise. No enemy, no matter how powerful, could or would destroy what God established. Sure, they would look around and see desolation, but when they did, they could remember the same God of old "who made a way through the sea, a path through the mighty waters, who drew out the chariots and horses, the army and reinforcements together, and [their enemies] lay there, never to rise again, extinguished, snuffed out like a wick" (Isaiah 43:16-17). It is indeed the same God who will also carry them and us toward life and liberation.

The reminder of the faithfulness and demonstrated power of God in the past is indeed a comfort, even to those of us today. Yet, before the nostalgia and the mindset of the good old days could set in, Isaiah abruptly says: "Forget the former things; do not dwell on the past. See, I am doing a new thing! Now it springs up; do you not perceive it? I am making a way in the wilderness and streams in the wasteland" (Isaiah 43:18-19).

It is with this same tension we too must walk forward asking God to show us the new things he has in store for us. We must ready ourselves to have the grapes of new wine poured into our new wineskins. We need to allow the timeless truth of God's heart, stewarded by those who have gone before us, to guide us as we pick up our mantle and walk forward. God affords new ways of doing things in and through us. We need to trust that despite the wastelands and deserts that we see as we walk, we too hold God's promises and should be ever perceiving the new springs, streams, and ways forward that he will provide.

MAKING ROOM FOR SOMETHING NEW

On June 23, 1840, Lucretia Mott arrived at the World Anti-Slavery Convention in London. For the three decades' prior,

England had been enacting legislation to end the slave trade, abolish slavery, and free around eight hundred thousand slaves throughout the British empire. Bringing together abolitionists from around the world to further the work of liberation was an important next step. Hundreds of delegates from around the world attended, including many Americans. Lucretia Mott was one of a handful of other women, including Elizabeth Cady Stanton, who intended to participate as delegates.

At that time Mott was a well-known and respected abolitionist. She had been speaking up and working to reverse the injustices of slavery in the United States for many years by the time she and her husband attended the 1840 London gathering. She boycotted slavery-produced goods and encouraged others to do the same. Alongside her husband she formed coalitions, hosted fugitive slaves, and raised and donated money to organizations that supported the abolition of slavery. So strong was her calling, leadership, and voice that she became a Quaker minister in 1821. Her Quaker faith taught and supported that God had created everyone equal, regardless of race, class, or gender. She used her platform to teach it.

When Mott walked into the convention in London with other women, they were not admitted. This was of no surprise to them as this male-only gathering had very specifically communicated that women were not welcome. The back-and-forth on the admittance of women took nearly a day to resolve, and finally the women were admitted but relegated to a women-only seating section and were unable to participate in any of the proceedings.[3]

That day Mott, aged forty-seven and a seasoned advocate, met Stanton, a twenty-five-year-old newlywed, and they agreed to begin to work together to add women's suffrage to their abolition efforts.[4] Not being able to attend a convention for equal rights and opportunities for slaves only highlighted the limited opportunities women also endured. Women were denied rights to their bodies and to their children, unable to own property, to work, earn, or keep their wages. Mott and Stanton birthed the US women's suffrage movement, and by 1848 they had organized and led the Seneca Falls Convention. This gathering was the first women's rights convention, where they drafted and recruited signers of the Declaration of Sentiments, a version of the Declaration of Independence writing women into the promises, privileges, and opportunities afforded those living in the United States.

Mott lived to see the end of slavery, as well as the passing of the fourteenth and fifteenth amendments affording Black men some opportunities during the reconstruction era after the Civil War. The nineteenth amendment, which afforded women the right to vote and set a path forward for the women's rights that I enjoy today, came about forty years after her death.

I often reflect on Lucretia Mott, a strong woman of faith who bravely and publicly shared messages that spoke against the cultural and political norms of her time. I think of the pushback that other people of faith (women included) must have given her, those who did not believe that a woman had the authority to speak against injustices like slavery or women's rights. I am inspired by her openness to work with someone new, young, and inexperienced like Stanton who was not defined by the same faith but by a shared moral argument that all of humanity was created equal. I am grateful for her courage and uncompromising conviction to hold hope and work hard for more than one issue and to not stop working until justice was present.

NEW SONGS TO CARRY US ON FORWARD

During the civil rights movement, which was being driven primarily by the Black Protestant church, Peter Scholtes, a White priest at St. Brendan's on the South Side of Chicago, was serving and leading a youth choir at his parish. Catholics at the time were just beginning to step into new practices of ecumenical work across Christian denominations after a history of teaching that any form of Christianity outside of Catholicism was heretical.

This new day of trying to work under the shared banner of the love of Christ was needed at every level as cries for civil rights for Black Americans were coming from across the country. Scholtes wanted his youth choir to sing a song that spoke to the faith and love needed in the moment. Finding none, one day he quickly penned his own and taught the youth to sing it:

> We are one in the Spirit. We are one in the Lord.
> And they'll know we are Christians by our love, by our love.[5]

Scholtes did not write the song to become famous or be seen. He had a youth choir to lead and brought what he could to a moment that was not centered around him. In joining what others were doing, he wrote a timeless truth of what could and should be.

To this day, his song has crossed religious, cultural, and generational lines, reminding the church that their unified public witness of love for each other testifies to the restorative work of Christ.[6]

Boldly joining together in song helps strip away the darkness of cynicism, fear, and small faith, bringing us toward a common hope of liberation, boundless love, and justice. But singing alone, no matter how true and powerful the message is, won't get us the justice we seek. Neither will friendships across racial lines.

Reading all the books on bridging racial divides won't get us there either.

It is going to take a joining up, a walking in. A realization that the status quo does not yield itself easily to those who have been intentionally written out of the system, and that only a reckoning to change it will. That reckoning does not start with individual movement in a familiar direction but instead happens when as individuals we join alongside communities and walk together toward change. The current of the status quo is deep and wide— its powerful movement will catch you and bring you along toward its confluence. Walking against those powerful currents of conformity and complacency is a long, important work. This is the work of resistance and the more people who join up, the more powerful the impact.

In walking out of the downstream current to join up with the stream of resistance, we need to learn new ways, sing new songs, follow new leaders, and draw from a deeper faith that will open our eyes to the restorative power of Christ. Our initial steps may feel unfamiliar and be tentative, but the longer we walk the more we realize the work is not for the faint of heart. We need to become brave.

"THEY'LL KNOW WE ARE CHRISTIANS BY OUR LOVE"

youtube.com/watch?v=LZg8Ho-lNqk

2

BRAVE STEPS

MARCHING FOR GEORGE FLOYD had begun to wind down. After all that had taken place in recent weeks to raise public awareness and demand change, people who had been working toward community solutions and policing reform were again at the table. City mayors, council members, and police were coming together with them in new ways to work toward substantive change.

During that time, a friend from Colorado Springs asked if she could come up to Denver to talk. She was beside herself with sadness and grief about all that was happening and the lack of care and concern from White Christians. She and her husband had lived as missionaries overseas for many years but for the past several years had been in the United States serving in senior leadership for a well-known Christian denomination.

I wasn't sure what a trip up to see me would do, but I agreed to have her come. She had reached a personal tipping point and whatever brave step she needed to take, she was ready to go. During our phone conversation, one thing she continued to say through her distress was that she needed to know what "to do" about all she was seeing.

WHAT DO I DO?

Over the years, in countless conversations, is the question, But what do I do? People who are waking up and beginning to care about injustice, but are outside of directly experiencing it, want to know. When the awareness of racial inequity and injustice begins to unfold, and the unsettling truth and reality of what is going on sets in, we ask: How can we fix this so it doesn't have to be this way?

This is a natural question that is good and problematic in several ways. It's good to see the pain and suffering of others— otherwise we wouldn't know there was a problem. As we walk into new levels of awareness and see the need for change, it is good we now desire to see and move toward doing something to make change. This is a good thing.

It's also problematic. The work of resistance does not begin when we see and step into it. The movement is bigger, deeper, and wider than this moment and our awareness of it. Whether we know them or not, others have been aware for a long time, share our desire for change, and are already working in big and small ways to make change. We need to learn the personal and collective history of those who have carried the water before us, then join them. We learn from their conviction, their courage, and their work. After the marching is over, we come back to their tables for the long, ongoing work of change.

We stand on the shoulders of those who have come before us. It is our job to ensure that we steward our season well and pass the torch to the next generation, leaving a good investment effort for others. This is the ongoing work of service—not to make a name for ourselves, not to build a social brand or identity on our knowledge, engagement, or greatness, but truly to serve alongside a present-day, faithful cloud of witnesses.

There's a lot more going on than what is initially seen, and it takes time to understand the problems. While we listen and center those voices closest to the pain, we serve and choose to become students. We live with an understanding that we must keep our eyes open to injustice's deep reality and efforts to alleviate it. The longer we stay, not trying to insert our solutions, the more we grow to understand solidarity alongside suffering.

Servants of the resistance know that one big solution, one fix to such a layered problem—aside from the return and implementation of a new kingdom—does not exist. We do what we can, and we don't stop, as though eradicating injustice was on a checklist or timeline. We come to understand that the problems are as layered as their solutions, some with unintended consequences yet to be seen. We come to understand that our questions of what we should "do" begin with service and the brave choice to walk humbly.

WALKING HUMBLY

The prophet Micah was a contemporary of Isaiah. Like Isaiah, he too spoke against the evil ways of Israel and Judah and warned of their future captivity. Amid obvious injustice and disregard for the heart of God and impending punishment, he also shared God's promised redemption. Micah was the prophet to predict that Jesus, the Redeemer, would be born in Bethlehem.

In the Bible, prophets were people who spoke on God's behalf. Seventeen of the thirty-nine books in the Old Testament were named after and written by prophets. Four prophets wrote five of the books, called the "major prophets" because they were so long, and twelve wrote small prophetic books called the "minor prophets." There are many more prophets throughout the Bible, from Abraham to John the Baptist, who didn't write books. Jesus too was referred to as a prophet on earth (John 7:4).

Prophets were known for both their foretelling and forthtelling. *Fore*telling speaks to revealing future events and *forth*telling speaks to the truth that God has already revealed. Much of what we think of regarding modern-day prophets is truth-telling what God has already revealed and reminding his people of the truth.

Prophets in the Bible were the truth-telling, ultimate resisters of their day. Bravely standing up to political and religious leaders, they held accountable those who did not reflect the concerns of God's heart or his intent for how people should be treated. Many were killed and tortured for their strong messages. Today's truth-tellers in the developed world are often allowed to live, but their message is met with resistance, and often discredited, discounted, and disregarded.

Micah lived in an agricultural community outside of political and religious powers of the day. Where he lived and what he saw may have been the reason he had deep concern for the poor and marginalized and why he pointed his message toward those in power in Jerusalem, the capital of Judah and Samaria, the capital of Israel.[1]

The church today often references the prophet Micah and his words as a central point of focus for the importance of doing justice work to please God. As a long-time justice doer, I am grateful for Micah's concise reminder: "He has shown you, O mortal, what is good. And what does the LORD require of you? To act justly and to love mercy and to walk humbly with your God" (Micah 6:8). I love the ESV, which actually says, "to do justice." While that is a powerful verse, the entire chapter sets the stage for the impact of its message.

The Lord is making his case against Israel. They have completely walked away from the heart of God. As God does this, he also calls them to remember their deliverance from Egypt, the journey and God's protection and deliverance to the Promised Land. As though in jest, using hyperbole, Micah shares a potential response for Israel to come back to the Lord.[2]

> With what shall I come before the LORD and bow down before the exalted God? Shall I come before him with burnt offerings, with calves a year old? Will the LORD be pleased with thousands of rams, with ten thousand rivers of olive oil? Shall I offer my firstborn for my transgression, the fruit of my body for the sin of my soul? (Micah 6:6-7)

What begins as small sacrifices to buy the Lord's favor—burnt offerings, calves that are a year old—become bigger. The bigger and more showy worship response—thousands of rams, ten thousand rivers of oil, the firstborn—becomes the absurd.

After listing such escalated, expensive gifts, Micah deescalates with "He has shown you . . ." (v. 8). God has demonstrated how to find our way back to God, and it's not something we can purchase. It is rekindling our hearts with the heart of God. To know God, to love God, is to see what he has shown us in his Word, how he set up systems, how he views all people, including the poor, the widow, the orphan, the slave. God has distinctly shown his justice and righteousness, and we are supposed to see, know, and do likewise.

First, mercy is a response to a problem. We see something. We feel something. We respond with immediate needs. Being a lover of mercy is hard. It means we never get tired and stop. No matter how many times we see someone in need of mercy, we are never finished showing it. Not only are we supposed to show mercy, but we are supposed to love doing it.

Second, justice recognizes there's a bigger picture than simply what we see and how we respond in the moment. A deeper look informs us how injustice came into place and does the necessary work to reverse and undo its harm. This reversal work is the essence of doing justice. *Mishpat*, the Hebrew word for justice, speaks to this restoration of the whole. Broader than individual restoration, it includes the restoration of societies and systems so everyone can live and act with peace.

Finally, God has shown us what is good and what he requires of us is to walk humbly. A perfect bookend to the earlier verses where anything but humility is suggested, this important, often under-utilized command is what makes all the difference.

Forgetting the ways of God, disregarding the cause of the poor, and creating a system that only looks out for ourselves and those who have power are completely against the heart of God. Yet, we see it all the time in our society, our houses of worship, and our homes. We sit, content to allow fires to burn both literally and figuratively. We keep ourselves at a comfortable distance sharing how it's just too big and overwhelming. We shut down. We try not to see. We say we leave it up to God but then we go on living as though it's not our problem. Here's the truth—it is our problem, and the only way to see it and move toward it is with humility.

Humility allows the enormity of injustice to move through our entire selves. It allows grief and lament to grip us. It provides us with a lens to recognize that all we think we are (good people) and all we think we have (good societies and systems) are often a result of exclusive efforts and greed. We can choose humility, gratitude, and conviction to change the status quo instead of becoming defensive, protective, and territorial. Brave steps forward mean we leave the comfort and privilege of the other side. It means we see the truth of God's heart, the ways in which humanity has gone astray, how we have gone astray. Brave steps are humble steps that intentionally choose to stay alongside those in need of change.

THE WAY OF CHRIST

The promise of the redemptive Christ in Micah is not our story but instead our history. We find our way to God through Christ, who being God took on the posture of a servant and became human, emptying himself of all his rights and privileges to make a just way forward (Philippians 2:7). He came with both humility and fire. He saw the truth of the world and spoke the heart of God into it. He prophetically helped to course correct the religious and political leaders of the day. He centered his work on the poor, the marginalized, and the vulnerable. I believe if we follow his example of humility and bravely step into our work, seeking to serve as he did, our loving mercy and doing justice might begin to work its way back toward his heart.

In following Jesus, we choose the humble way—emptying ourselves of our power and established place—join the people on the margins, always love mercy, and do the long, hard work of justice. True service requires the bravery of choosing to be humble, to recognize the movement has not been waiting for us to show up to demand attention. The movement needs our body, our solidarity, and our service. Intentionally choosing a humble place of service will result in a place of true honor and effective work.

Jesus was invited into a Pharisee's house, and he noticed that the guests sought out seats of honor. Then Jesus shared the following parable:

When someone invites you to a wedding feast, do not take the place of honor, for a person more distinguished than you may have been invited. If so, the host who invited both of you will come and say to you, "Give this person your seat." Then, humiliated, you will have to take the least important place. But when you are invited, take the lowest place, so that when your host comes, he will say to you, "Friend, move up to a better place." Then you will be honored in the presence of all the other guests. *For all those who exalt themselves will be humbled, and those who humble themselves will be exalted.* (Luke 14:8-11, emphasis added)

Jesus followed up the parable with instructions to the host:

When you give a luncheon or dinner, do not invite your friends, your brothers or sisters, your relatives, or your rich neighbors; if you do, they may invite you back and so you will be repaid. But when you give a banquet, invite the poor, the crippled, the lame, the blind, and you will be blessed. Although they cannot repay you, you will be repaid at the resurrection of the righteous. (Luke 14:12-14)

Inviting those who are marginalized, centering their presence, will be a blessing but not in the way that gives you what you thought. The way of Jesus is the way of the resistance, and it takes courage to make brave moves away from human power and toward humbly being lovers of mercy and doers of justice.

All of this and more was what I had in mind when I was considering my friend from Colorado Springs when she wanted to *do* something in the wake of George Floyd.

As we talked, I encouraged her to decenter herself, her guilt, and her panic and find people who were doing the work to undo harmful racial oppression, like the NAACP. I knew her hometown had an active chapter. I told her to walk in with a large check to fund their work and supplies to clean the bathroom. "Tell them you are ready to serve and support what they are doing, from cleaning the bathrooms to whatever else is needed. In a humble and generous posture, offer your body, your time, and your resources." I would never want to put someone who cleans offices out of their job, but the meaning of the message I was sharing was she could do something, if it was humble, generous, and of service.

I followed up with her a year and a half later and asked if she did what I suggested. While she told me she did not walk in to the NAACP, she did tell me she reached out to a Black woman she knew who was serving the community with a small nonprofit on the side. She offered the suggested support and did anything this woman asked, from helping to clean out a deceased relative's house to eventually sitting on her nonprofit board as the only White participant.

She told me:

[While I sat, served, and listened] I learned so much. I may not have done things the same way, but I learned and supported. A lot of trust was built, so were mutual connections. A year later, because of our deeper work together, the nonprofit was able to build connections through a friend of mine and one thing led to another. June 2020 that nonprofit led the city's Juneteenth celebration efforts and paid no fees.

By doing what I was asked, I earned trust and the opportunity to support her community's voice in ways I couldn't have imagined. My family had a big move to Ohio recently, but that experience changed everything I am seeing and doing today.

It takes bravery to move beyond tears of guilt into true tears of lament and shared solidarity, to decenter what we want to do and humbly join others in the work they are doing. Serving the movement means we give humbly and generously of our time, money, and resources with gratitude that we can help carry the water a little farther up the hill. Doing the work of resistance is a long work; it's hard to consistently submit to its length. Not only that but it's hard to submit to being in a serving posture that long without recognition. Here's the raw truth, you never stop serving the movement and that takes real courage.

STEPPING UP THE BRAVE

In 2014 I had the opportunity to lead a border trip for pastors and nonprofit leaders. Thousands of unaccompanied minors had come to the border to seek asylum, and the government was unable to meet the demands. Wanting to see things firsthand, I called my boss and asked if we could go. He was more than glad to jump in and connected me with his uncle, Frank Castellanos, who lived in the McAllen/Brownville, Texas, area. He was well-connected and a hidden gem in his community. His small community had moved to front page news, and he and others were working to meet the immediate needs of people in hard circumstances and were learning how to allow themselves to grow with the pressure.

One of those community leaders was Sister Norma Pimentel. Sister Norma ran Catholic Charities of the Rio Grande Valley (CCRGV). She was humble, hard-working, and an amazing collaborator. When the kids kept coming, she pulled together a resource center housed in CCRGV with support from different denominations and public sectors. She was efficient, well-respected, and not one to seek any attention. Frank told me that if we were headed there, we had to meet Sister Norma.

I called her nonprofit and asked if we could meet her and hear what she was doing. Her staff answered. "Yes, you can come and see the work, but Sister Norma doesn't like to speak to groups."

We arrived with our group of more than forty leaders and saw firsthand how her leadership had assembled private, nonprofit, and public sector collaboration to meet the needs of thousands of families and children seeking asylum. It was beyond impressive. We were not in the building ten minutes when we were asked to gather in an area and wait. After an awkward wait, Sister Norma came out and began to share. As she began her humble, quiet narrative, I knew we were in the presence of a modern-day saint. We listened to her assessment of what was going on and how we could help support the collective work and, most importantly, the impacted families.

It did not take long for people to call me after the trip to ask what could be learned. I remember telling Ivone Gullien, who was leading the immigration initiatives at Sojourners at the time, that they needed to invite Sister Norma to their annual conference as a speaker, she was so insightful and inspiring; she was on the front lines doing the work and learning from her was a must.

After that time, I would see Sister Norma on Capitol Hill, in the news meeting the Pope, testifying for the United Nations. I was always so grateful for her willingness to put herself out there and tell the stories of what she was seeing. I also thought about that time so many years ago when getting her to come out of her office to share her perspective with outside groups was a stretch.

I found myself leading another border trip to McAllen, Texas, in the fall of 2018. Different group, different administration, same issues but with the additional layer of separating children from their families at the border. I headed back to CCRGV to meet up with Sister Norma. She was the same humble woman, filled with conviction and compassion, but she was also more out front.

During her question-and-answer time, I reminded her of our first meeting. "Sister Norma, four years ago, when your organization became front page, national news, you did not like to talk to outside people. So much has changed. I see you all over, speaking up. What changed?"

She smiled and did not miss a beat. "I realized that I needed to become braver. I needed to grow and stretch and put myself out in front of others so those impacted by pain and suffering could have their stories told. By telling their stories to people in power, church leaders, and media they can have better opportunities."

To this day you can find Sister Norma, a globally known Catholic nun, at the McAllen border inspiring volunteers, crossing into Mexico to support immigrants in migrant camps, posting stories on Facebook, and speaking out on issues that support change for immigrants. She does not just do the work and tell those in her comfortable circles but continues to be published in national media sources and meet with global leaders, ever advocating for justice. Sister Norma has not made her work or public voice about her. She always centers the story of migrants and our shared need to support them with the hands and feet of Christ, always working toward justice.

Serving the movement is not about centering ourselves or even the leaders of the movement we are joining. It is about centering those who are directly impacted and ensuring that their voices, needs, and stories are shared. Those of us who have chosen to join up with them need to make sure that we are willing to serve in places and ways that center the struggle, stretch beyond our comfort zone, and work toward a hopeful vision. This hopeful vision is a brave choice to work toward what can and should be. In our service we proclaim things as they should be, and sometimes that proclamation of resistance is in song.

SONG AS RESISTANCE

As a musician and worship leader, singing hopeful songs of resistance is both a spiritual practice and a way of life to me. Some weeks we sing alongside the pain and brokenness of our individual and collective lives. We rejoice that a Savior has come; we weep that another human tragedy has occurred—so many emotions cried out together in our shared yet hopeful struggle. With a purely human and logical lens, it simply makes no sense.

With our shared hope of Christ, who has liberated humanity from death and dying and is coming again, Christians continue to sing a vision of what can be. We sing of our history. We sing our praise. We sing our hallelujahs to God. We sing those hallelujahs with and to each other. In singing praise amid death and dying, we are raising a song of resistance. May his kingdom come, may his will be done on earth as it is in heaven.

This simple but powerful practice has been passed down in humanity's lineage, and it is no surprise that art and song have played a major role in the work of resistance. Secular or sacred, singing our struggle is healing. Singing our hope provides direction.

I recently had the opportunity to join Dr. James A. Forbes as he shared the importance of song in the work of resistance. He grew up and walked into the fight for civil rights in the United States in the 1960s. Dr. Forbes was the first African American

senior pastor of the largest multicultural and multidenomina-
tional church, Riverside Church in Manhattan, New York. He is a
long-standing community and national leader who has con-
tributed greatly to the work of racial and economic justice.

In sharing with our intimate group of Christian justice leaders,
he both talked and sung his way through his lecture. "Songs provided survival. The music was therapeutic. Singing brought us
through." He went on to share how God had given the song "We
Shall Overcome" to the movement. He laughed as he reminisced
about the confidence with which they sang in the face of what
looked like anything but overcoming.

In singing songs of resistance in the midst of oppression, he
said, "That music was actually depositing the kind of vitamin to
sustain us during these times." In the brave, ongoing work of
service, we too need to deposit vitamins that will sustain us and
drive us forward. Bravely joining in song helps strip away the
darkness of cynicism, fear, and small faith, bringing us toward a
common hope of liberation, boundless love, and justice.

LIFT EVERY VOICE AND SING

On President Abraham Lincoln's birthday, February 12, thirty-
five years after his death, five hundred Jacksonville, Mississippi,
schoolchildren in the segregated Stanton School sang a poem
written by their principal and local NAACP leader, James Weldon
Johnson.[3] His brother John Rosamond Johnson wrote the music.
James later recalled:

> Shortly afterwards my brother and I [James Weldon
> Johnson] moved away from Jacksonville to New York, and
> the song passed out of our minds. But the school children

of Jacksonville kept singing it; they went off to other schools and sang it; they became teachers and taught it to other children. Within twenty years it was being sung over the South and in some other parts of the country. . . . The lines of this song repay me in an elation, almost of exquisite anguish, whenever I hear them sung by Negro children.[4]

This song, "Lift Every Voice and Sing," with its clear vision for the future, quickly moved through the Black community. It was named the Black National Anthem in 1919 by the NAACP, twelve years before "The Star-Spangled Banner" became the national anthem. "Lift Every Voice and Sing" has been heralded as "an omnipresent part of African American worship traditions and an enduring refrain for great Black artists."[5]

Lift every voice and sing,
'Til earth and heaven ring,
Ring with the harmonies of Liberty. . . .
God of our weary years,
God of our silent tears,
Thou who has brought us thus far on the way;
Thou who has by Thy might
Led us into the light,
Keep us forever in the path, we pray. . . .
May we forever stand.[6]

Powerful, beautiful lyrics, sung with conviction, reminding of where they had been and where they hoped to go, was passed from one hopeful singer of resistance to another, deeply depositing vitamins to carry them during a Jim Crow South.

Forty years after those school children sang, at a Black school's eighth-grade graduation in Arkansas, a White commencement speaker hurried in and out to deliver a commencement speech to the Black audience of graduating students and their families. Instead of celebrating accomplishments and sharing a vision of their bright future ahead, the speaker informed the community of all the investments that would be coming to Central High School, the local White school where these students were unable to attend. This man was running for a local election and cared little of those he might be representing. After he spoke, he left with his colleague, the only other White person in the auditorium. "The ugliness they left was palpable."[7]

Following that pitiful and painful commencement speaker, the planned program continued. A hymn was performed and the poem "Invictus" was orated by the class.[8] The final words of the poem—"I am the master of my fate. I am the captain of my soul"— could not have felt more untrue after the commencement speaker projected the lack of future he saw in the students and families sitting before him.

The class valedictorian, Henry Reed, stood up to begin his commencement address. He had chosen Hamlet's soliloquy "To Be or Not to Be" to orate. As he spoke, "his voice rose on tides of promise and fell on waves of warnings." One of his classmates listened, "silently rebutting each sentence with [her] eyes closed." The pain of what had taken place on that day was so strong she could not believe a different future for anyone.

But after Henry had finished, something happened:

There was a hush, which in an audience warns that something unplanned is happening. . . . Henry Reed, the conservative, the proper, the A student, turn[ed] his back to the audience and turn[ed] to us (the proud graduating class of 1940) and [sang] nearly speaking,

> Lift every voice and sing,
> 'Till earth and heaven ring,
> Ring with the harmonies of Liberty . . .

The students, parents, and guests sang together and "joined the hymn of encouragement." And,

> while echoes of the song shivered in the air, Henry Reed bowed his head, said "thank you" and returned to his place in the line. The tears that slipped down many faces were not wiped away in shame. We were on top again. As always, again. We survived. The depths had been ice and dark, but now a bright sun spoke to our souls. I was no longer simply a member of the proud graduating class of 1940; I was a proud member of the wonderful, beautiful Negro race.[9]

The truth of these words, sung boldly in the face of oppression, low expectations, and white supremacy, sang truth in the face of power and helped move one of Henry's classmates from cynicism to a place of Black community pride. That classmate was Maya Angelou. This and many other stories of her formation are in her memoir, *I Know Why the Caged Bird Sings*.

Dare to bravely sing songs of victory in the face of oppression. To resist the reality of what is and,

> Out of the gloomy past,
> 'Til now we stand at last
> Where the white gleam of our bright star is cast
> God of our weary years,
> God of our silent tears,
> Thou who has brought us thus far on the way;
> Thou who hast by Thy might
> Led us into the light

Keep us forever in the path. . . .

Shadowed beneath Thy hand,

May we forever stand,

True to our God,

True to our native land.[10]

"LIFT EVERY VOICE AND SING/BLACK NATIONAL ANTHEM"

youtube.com/watch?v=ko3LdleyOQs

3

FALLING FORWARD

IN 1962, A SMALL BLACK WOMAN, alongside seventeen other willing people from Sunflower County in the Mississippi Delta, boarded a bus headed to the local county courthouse. All had recently attended a meeting at a church in Ruleville, Mississippi, where they learned that as US citizens they had the right to vote.

Fannie Lou Hamer, who had been working on a share-cropping plantation since she was a child, had never known that her vote was possible. She had never heard of civil rights, but having lived in the Jim Crow South, she understood why change was needed. She knew that if people like her could vote, then sparks for change could happen. Those who were in power and laws that kept her community in perpetual fear and oppression could be eradicated. At that church gathering, when invited to go to the courthouse and register to vote, she felt like it was a calling from God. She willingly raised her hand and set off a series of events that would change her life and the life of Black people in Mississippi forever.

As the history has been told repeatedly, Ms. Hamer and everyone on that bus were denied the opportunity to register to vote that day. Given obscure questions, as well as identifying ones so that when they registered their employers and community would know, the registrar's office used fear and intimidation to keep people from registering. But the seed of determination that was birthed that day in Ms. Hamer compelled her to keep trying. After her third attempt, she was able to register successfully. This huge victory, however, came with enormous consequences. She had to flee from her home, she was fired from her job, shot at while she slept, and threatened. Enormous personal and family sacrifice only increased over time, yet she persevered.

Ms. Hamer began to get noticed by other leaders in the civil rights movement, and it wasn't long before the Student Non-violent Coordinating Committee (SNCC) hired her to work throughout the state, registering other Black people to vote. Her work changed the face of voting and equality for Black Americans.

Once she and others had earned the federal protection needed to vote through the Voting Rights Act, she continued to work to see Black people on voting ballots, even running for the US House (she did not win). She continued to work toward changing systems so that people were not subjected to poverty. By 1972, 62.2 percent of the state's eligible Black voters were on the rolls, ten times as many as in 1964 before she began.[1]

Hamer felt the sweetness of meeting her goal of personally registering to vote and continued forward doing whatever else was necessary for shared liberation for Black people in Mississippi. Ms. Hamer knew the cost of her activism, but she was not going to back down: "Sometimes it seem like to tell the truth today is to run the risk of being killed. But if I fall, I'll fall five feet four inches forward in the fight for freedom. I'm not backing off."[2]

NOT BACKING OFF

After over a decade of living, working, and worshiping in my community as a teacher, church worship leader, and nonprofit program staffer, I had come to a new plateau in my personal awareness and engagement of unjust systems. It seemed that no matter how hard we all worked together on our personal and shared growth, our flourishing was limited by structural, systemic barriers. I became very frustrated at what felt like the futility of our efforts. The systems designed to work for many were flat out not working for my community. It was time to reevaluate our approach; it was time for me to reevaluate mine.

I did not want to quit my day job, but I knew I needed to get smarter and better at understanding how to impact what was holding our community back. I asked a lot of questions of people in community development work, law, and public policy. I wanted help and direction because our community needed more support. Seeing the pain, feeling the urgency of injustice, and spinning around trying to figure out what to do with it all left me asking God where to place my next steps.

Having three little kids in tow, anything but daily survival seemed a little ridiculous—we were about as stretched as we could be as a family of five with young children. There was always more work than time, more need than money, but I just could not let it rest. We needed to effectively address systems alongside the other important social issues facing our community. We needed to grow, and more specifically, I needed to grow.

It seemed like my husband, David, and I were both talking about systems and our leadership limitations a lot at this point. I remember one day sharing with him, "Why don't you go to law school? You are so smart. You could go to night school. I will happily care for our kids." My noble wife and mother voice was so inspiring that he paused a moment to think about it.

Just as I thought we might have a conversation about my proposal, he stopped abruptly and responded, "I don't want to go to law school. I like my job. You go to law school. Stop living your dreams through me."

Frankly, I was shocked at his response. It was so definitive. Up until this point we had been doing work and life in the same lane. I wanted to expand my lane and though he also needed to better understand and impact oppressive laws and systems, it wasn't his lane that needed a drastic change, it was mine.

"Living my dreams through him." Was that what I was doing? The daily life of family and work hadn't completely snuffed out my wick of individuality, but had it caused me to limit what God might be doing in me specifically? It was time for me to walk a little more deeply and go a little more solo into this next chapter.

Not a year later, I had taken the GRE and was enrolled in night school at the University of Colorado at Denver to begin studying public policy and administration. I was so glad to be learning about the systems that I had worked in for years as an educator and social service system of support. It was like all these lights began to come on for me; I was seeing and learning the back end of the machine and not just dealing with its output.

Not everyone needs to formalize their learning and get a master's degree in public policy to make an impact on systemic barriers, but everyone who is in the work needs to push themselves to bring what they have in smarter, more effective ways. For me, a formal education to unite my experience and passion was the exact right place, and as I moved forward, God continued to confirm my new steps, driving me deeper.

NEW STEPS, DEEPER DIVE

During that season, everywhere I turned God was confirming that I was headed in the right direction. I needed those constant confirmations because faith in myself and in my contribution was small. Standing alongside my community at the deepest grassroots level had grown so comfortable, learning new formal skills to bring to our collective table felt both unfamiliar and intimidating.

One of those confirmations was when I attended the annual Christian Community Development Association (CCDA) conference, in the fall of 2005. My husband had been faithfully attending for years; we had been living out the CCDA philosophy of ministry for well over a decade. Having babies and limited resources kept me at home, but every year David would ask me to join him. I finally decided to go, and it was a great experience. I was surrounded by thousands of people who were living out our shared philosophy of ministry. Each speaker and worship song that was sung, I received as bread for the journey of the work. I was so grateful to be there.

It seemed like at every plenary session they talked about social justice and systemic barriers, further confirming my direction the past few years. After a series of days, David said, "You picked the right conference to attend. I have never heard so much about confronting unjust systems in all my years attending. This is great for you, Michelle, but it is also unusual." I didn't care what had happened before, the message I was hearing was meeting me where I was. I had a tribe, and I was going to keep learning alongside them.

The presenters were a diverse array of people from different ages and races, with a balance of men and women. During the final night of presenters, an older White man took to the stage. He talked about politics in a very confrontational way. I had never heard someone be that bold. Politics and church were lines that had never been crossed, even in my little church in the city. What he shared might have made some uncomfortable, but this audience knew all too well the injustice of laws and policies that favored the privileged and gave little regard to the poor.

He not only made a case for raising our collective voice, but he shared about an upcoming federal budget that was set to cut resources in food security, housing, and healthcare. I was so hungry for what he shared; I had been painfully closing in on that culturally drawn line between politics and religion. I was ready to jump over but needed some leadership to inspire and help me over the final hurdles.

After his sermon, he invited those who were interested to join him in Washington, DC, a month later to protest what he referred to as an "immoral budget." When the session was over and the informal meeting for those interested was initiated, I think I was the first one up front. This was the church altar call I had been waiting for.

A month later I was on a plane with my husband. We left our three kids in the care of a dear friend, and we participated in our first civil disobedience action. That December day was absolutely freezing; I cannot remember a day when I have ever been physically colder. Bundled in layers and layers, we set out to meet with our legislators from Colorado before we met up with the larger group. In our senator's office we talked about our experiences and our disappointments in the system. We shared, they listened. It was the first time I had ever met with someone from a US senator's office. I went with stories and conviction, but all the while I felt insecure; I was underdressed; I seemed small and ill-equipped. I did it anyway.

The next day we met up at Lutheran Church of the Reformation, a church located less than two blocks from the Capitol. There we listened to speakers, sang songs of hope, and then did "civil disobedience arrest training" in the aisles of the sanctuary. Being a worship leader, I was familiar with filling the aisles of a worship service, but never had I experienced such a radical display of worship. Training on how to be arrested, how not to resist arrest, and other pertinent skills were on full display. We were preparing.

A large group of about one hundred walked to the steps of the Cannon House, an austere marble building that houses congressional offices. On full display, pastors and ministry leaders from around the country who were living, working, and worshiping in poor communities protested the upcoming budget. We chanted and sang as we walked the few blocks together. We listened and clapped to the inspiring colleagues who spoke. We sat down on the ice-cold steps of the Cannon House Building and blocked an entrance until we were arrested.

I have numerous memories of that day—marching together, getting arrested, being detained, and meeting new people that became future allies and mentors in my faith-rooted activism journey. I learned so much during that trip, both about myself and simple, practical things for my future work. I was grateful, deeply grateful.

One thing that really stood out to me was what God put on my heart to bring to our experience. As a worship leader, I was walking our church through the current Advent season, and songs of the season were in my heart and mind. It was not lost on me that the celebration of Light breaking forth in darkness with the arrival of Jesus was during this time, and the third verse of "O Holy Night" was running on a mental loop. We had been encouraged to come to the event with prayers and words to pray and bring. That's what the Spirit was giving me to offer.

It was loud and chaotic with a hundred or so people all talking out. Once we sat down to block the entrance, everyone was pretty much on their own. I was scared and embarrassed to speak out and share anything. I had never done anything like this before, yet in the middle of a group of well-known evangelicals such as Shane Claiborne, Brian McLaren, Mary Nelson, Jim Wallis, John Perkins, and others, I sat on my knees and sang. I sang in a posture of prayer the truth and hope that God had been whispering to my soul in that moment:

> Truly he taught us to love one another.
> His law is love and his gospel is peace.
> Chains shall he break, for the slave is our brother;
> And in his name all oppression shall cease.
> Sweet hymns of joy in grateful chorus raise we;
> With all our hearts we praise his holy name.
> Christ is the Lord! O, praise his name forever.
> His power and glory ever more proclaim![3]

It took time to process what I had just joined. I had left my kids with a friend, wondering how long I would be in jail; I wondered if my efforts would have any impact on our shared current reality. Back home, I shared my experience with people in person, at events, and in the media. I spoke at one of the local United Methodist churches in Denver, and while they embraced it, others began to challenge what they viewed as "political" actions.

Amid all this new public sharing, I did a lot of internal reflection and came to understand that this public action was not "political," but rather a prophetic, public witness. It was a line I was drawing in the sand that silence in the face of injustice was no longer an option for me. I grew new roots through that experience, coming to understand that part of the power of protest is how it steadies and emboldens the voice of the one protesting, in this case me. I was not going to be concerned with how I was perceived—if the Spirit had things to speak through me, I was going to speak, or sing, them boldly. Injustice would not be fixed from a sideline or even in quiet participation. This was a bold, forward-facing work of resistance.

ACTIVISM AND RESISTANCE

Walking into resistance begins in the mind, an awakening to the realization that without confrontation and public action, the status quo will never change. We cannot live life with the same old mindset—we need to cross over and boldly step into new levels of work. We perceive that God is doing a new thing in us and in his overall work in this moment, and now we need to bravely walk in.

Brave steps are needed, not just because we think we need to do something new, but because our minds and hearts need to be reoriented toward humble service that takes courage. We need to ensure our motives are in the right place, that we know how to empty ourselves and join the work of walking humbly and serving those who are leading and working toward resistance.

Activism is not something that stays in the mind or the heart, but it moves through the whole body driving it forward, ensuring that things do not remain as they are. Often we think of activism as participation in public, radical events, even to the point of civil disobedience and arrests. These are activities that activists do, but activism is full-body engagement in other ways also, to change the current social reality; it's actively working toward change. Activism is demanding, forward-driven motion. It is active, full-scale public witness, not done on social media, although social media can tell the story of movement and call toward change. It is embracing and participating in the physical work necessary to make change.

Full-scale public witness, however, is met with resistance, not only in the public square but in our social circles, our relationships, and even our own minds. This resistance can be helpful—it enables us to root down and own the evolving conviction we are walking into. When I speak of resistance, I am not thinking about anger or public displays of hostility; I am thinking of *friction*, the ability to rub up against something and effectively move forward.

Without giving a deep physics lesson, this is an important principle from the physical world. Friction is essential for effective movement. Simple walking cannot take place until our feet come in contact with the ground; friction keeps us from slipping and falling. It provides heat and traction, keeping us from slipping around in harmful directions. Bringing our ideas outside of our minds and on public display is met with sometimes very helpful friction.

We need some friction to help form our thoughts more clearly and outside of a vacuum. Pushing back and forth on ideas, solutions, history, and experiences is the exact back-and-forth that democracy is hinged on—we the people, *all* the people, work together toward good solutions for everyone. When only a select few make the decisions for the masses, those who are harmed by those decisions need collective voice to speak up for change. This is the essence of resistance and friction's natural work. It's not a bad thing, and it's an important process. In our faith circles, we often hear a similar reference: "As iron sharpens iron, so one person sharpens another" (Proverbs 27:17).

Though friction is effective, too much friction can be ineffective.[4] This is an important parallel in resistance work. Too much friction can cause unwanted heat, creating greater wear and tear or resulting in fire. Too much friction can lead to less efficiency and an inability to move at all. Additionally, too much friction can create higher levels of noise that cause people to shut off the cause of the friction indefinitely.

This is basic science. Resistance and pushback are needed to shape a better outcome, but too much can be destructive. As you consider falling forward with more conviction, keep in mind that neither the work nor those we are trying to influence need someone who does not regulate their levels of resistance. It's a balance to be heard and be a positive influence for change.

TOO MUCH FRICTION

A few years ago, asylum seekers were coming to the US borders and being detained. Asylum is a legal way to gain entrance to the United States: those who come to our border and prove they have a credible threat to their lives because of religious or political persecution in their country of origin are allowed to make a case to the US government to stay, free from harm, in the United States.

The administration at that time, however, was referring to this globally agreed-upon law and the migrants who were utilizing it as unlawful, and immediately and without exception detaining migrants for indefinite periods of time in immigrant detention facilities. This new posture toward asylum seekers caused a lot of resistance throughout our country.

Immigration facilities became overcrowded. Entire families with children were detained and places designed to hold a few hundred were double and triple their capacity. Across the country, this narrative and practice were decried. Immigrant's rights groups came together to join what was referred to as "Lights for Liberty." Over seven hundred cities hosted events.[5] In my city, Denver, our event was held at an immigrant detention center in Aurora.

Bringing a couple of young people from the community with me, we headed over to the vigil. Over one thousand people were gathered, listening to stories, poems, songs from those who were directly impacted by the detention center. As I walked through the crowd, I greeted longtime friends and allies. Here we were, like so many other times, rallying for justice for immigrants. It was a time of shared solidarity and healing as well as hope for a new day for justice.

Alongside our group was another group who shared our frustrations with the government. Instead of staying close to the rally outside the ICE detention center's property, they began to walk over toward the facility, and it escalated from there. Some took down the American flag on the property and replaced it with a Mexican flag and placed other signs that denigrated the police and law enforcement. Our group began to disband as the event escalated in a direction that was not shared.

Media that had come to tell the story of our shared message and peaceful protest were now crossing lines into the facility and covering this small group of agitators. Theirs was the message that would be told and taken to task on social media by city officials, the governor, and US House members.[6] Partisan lines were drawn and the conversation about desecrating the flag was headlined. All our good efforts were now being discredited because of this small group.

Several of my friends were interviewed about what happened that night. The two groups had met before the event to ensure that both could work together. After, there was frustration around a misalignment with tactics and shared outcomes, but they came together to see how they could try again in the future.

The work of the movement took an unfortunate step sideways that night because of too much friction. Yet everyone brushed themselves off, regrouped, and held a welcoming posture for future work together. A longtime friend and immigration activist who has been living in sanctuary in a Denver church for years, Jeanette Vizguerra, wanted everybody who was involved in the protest to move on: "We're calling for unity. We welcome any ally, any person that wants to join the movement," she said.[7]

I have a lot of respect for leaders like Jeanette who, in the face of unintended outcomes, are willing to demonstrate and hold an open posture to come together and try again. She, like so many other leaders, understands that for movements to grow, others need to be invited in and be united. Efforts, especially as they grow, always face potential fracturing, which is why hers is an important posture to hold.

NOT BY MIGHT

The summer after I had graduated with my policy degree, I was raring to go. I had formalized my education and had grown in understanding on how government systems worked and how to impact them for change. In addition to classroom learning, I had been practicing my new, emerging skills and making stronger connections in the public sector. I felt prepared, eager, and open to whatever was in store for my immediate future.

At that time, I was invited to join a cohort of other community development leaders from around the country. They were an impressive, experienced group of people: social workers, teachers, pastors, nonprofit leaders. All of us shared a Christian faith and commitment to join the work of restorative justice alongside our communities. It was great to be with so many like-minded people, and it was also exactly the reminder I needed after all that formal training—ours was a work of the Spirit, of faith, and not of human effort alone.

At one of our gatherings, we listened to an elder in the movement share about his work for over four decades as a pastor and educator in New York City. He spoke of the need to depend on Christ; then he stopped, looked at me directly, and said, "And it's not going to be by might and it's not going to be by power. It's going to be by my Spirit, said the Lord." He was quoting from the book of Zechariah, and while he did not choose to look at me for any particular reason, I sensed that message was for me and internalized it deeply.

The next day we heard another inspiring elder in the movement share about his church and community development project in Chicago. As though he had notes from the day before, during his talk he stopped, looked at me directly, and said, "And it's not going to be by might and it's not going to be by power. It's going to be by my Spirit, said the Lord." At that point, I knew that message was for me. God wanted me to understand that in the work he was calling me to do, all my new equipping skills would be helpful, but this was the work of his Spirit.

Two weeks later, I had an allergic reaction to a drug that left me fighting for my life. The systemic reaction was so hard to control that by the time it finally stopped I was extremely frail. It would take months to regain my strength and be able to engage any type of work beyond caring for myself and my young family. When I did begin again, it felt like small steps of rebuilding.

God had been reminding me up front that the work I was stepping up into was not going to be a result of my own power or new skills. In case I had missed it, he was going to allow me the opportunity to feel the loss of my own physical power and watch him rebuild his work in me.

The prophet Zechariah lived many years after Isaiah and Micah. The Jewish people had been in exile for seventy years and now, under the new Persian empire, those who had been exiled under Babylonian rule were returning to their home countries. Being polytheistic, the Persian ruler wanted to reestablish houses of worship to all the gods of the people who had been held captive.

Many of the exiled Jews returned to a place they had never known, while others had faint memories of how things used to be. Zechariah served as God's voice to the people as they returned and rebuilt their home country. During this time of rebuilding, Zechariah is shown many visions and given direct words of inspiration to comfort the returning exiles.

Zerubbabel was one of those returning Jewish exiles and the governor of Judah. He was given authority and resources from Persia to rebuild the temple in Jerusalem. We learn a bit about this process through the books of Ezra and Nehemiah, but in Zechariah chapter four, Zechariah shares a vision given as a direct word of encouragement from the Lord to Zerubbabel, this civic leader: "'Not by might nor by power, but by my Spirit,' says the LORD Almighty" (Zechariah 4:6).

Zerubbabel is promised that he will lead a successful effort until the final capstone is laid—his is not going to be an effort in futility. It will be completed and he will share in the joy of the finished product. Despite destruction, loss, and an enormously long job, God encourages him to keep moving forward. His is a work of the Spirit, not of the Persian authority, or even capable, civic leaders like the governor of Judah! God would once again demonstrate his might and show his glory by growing things in ways that humans cannot explain. And, in direct contrast to his power and majesty, God poses this question: "Who dares despise the day of small things?" (Zechariah 4:10).

God is not containable and what appear to be "small things" should not be despised or limited. The work of God's Spirit is the fuel for restoration and healing. He will accomplish what he purposes. In taking what we are given, we see how God multiplies the work of his kingdom.

SMALL THINGS

Jesus was faithfully stewarding the message of the kingdom when he shared these parables in Matthew:

> "The kingdom of heaven is like a mustard seed, which a man took and planted in his field. Though it is the smallest of all seeds, yet when it grows, it is the largest of garden plants and becomes a tree, so that the birds come and perch in its branches."
>
> He told them still another parable: "The kingdom of heaven is like yeast that a woman took and mixed into about sixty pounds of flour until it worked all through the dough." (Matthew 13:31-33)

The good work of kingdom restoration, whether done in a sacred or secular setting, is a deeply spiritual work; do not minimize the humble, small efforts that you and others bring to it. Whether it is building or rebuilding, allow God to take your small offerings and plant them into his bigger kingdom work that defies human logic and is eternal.

Let the work lead you with shouts of joy, like the people alongside the work of rebuilding the temple with Zerubbabel—"God bless it! God bless it!" (Zechariah 4:7). Allow the small acts, with small faith, to move mountains, not by your might or power but by his Spirit.

BEYOND ONE DAY

Viola Liuzzo was the only White woman killed in the civil rights movement. She served the movement. She was not content to read about injustice, nor did she use excuses to explain why she should stay home with other White women and allow history to move forward without her efforts.

Viola's engagement and work with the NAACP grew out of a close friendship she had with a Black woman she met at a grocery store. In 1964, Viola participated in protests in her hometown of Detroit. Martin Luther King Jr., who joined them, called for all people of faith to come help down in Alabama during the 1964 Selma to Montgomery marches, because "it was everybody's fight."[8]

Viola heard his request and went to Selma to do her part, volunteering and supporting those who were joining together for the several-days march. On March 25, 1964, over twenty-five thousand people came to the Montgomery, Alabama, capitol building to fight for voting rights. Viola spent much of that day helping to shuttle people from Montgomery back to the starting point in Selma. This is no small effort and one many people might not realize is a need. But when you march for miles, you want a car to bring you back to the starting point because you are tired and need to be driven. Viola was one of those important drivers, supporting the legs of weary marchers.

During one of those back-and-forth shuttles, the KKK shot into her car and murdered her. It was sheer hate for the efforts she was making that got her killed. Those who killed her were disgusted by Black people asserting their rights and anyone who supported them, even a White housewife and mother from Detroit.

Her murder was national news and remembered as an important part of getting the Voting Rights Act passed. During the evolving story, the FBI and those investigating started a smear campaign accusing Viola of being a drug addict and having an affair with a Black man—as though that would justify her senseless death. An autopsy revealed the FBI's smear campaign was not true, but this information was not uncovered until 1978, fourteen years later.

You can see markers of her contribution along US Highway 80, twenty miles east of Selma, and in Detroit at the Viola Liuzzo Park Association, where a statue was dedicated in June 2019.[9]

HOLD ON

At this point in our journey of joining, we are coming to understand that falling forward means we have not created an exit plan but are fully committed to the uphill, unglamorous work of resistance. For some it may be full-time like Fannie Lou Hamer, for others it might be some act of service for a day or week like Viola

Liuzzo. We remain inspired by the faith of those who have gone before us and done the internal, committed work necessary to add and not distract from the movement.

We have chosen to become students and servants of the resistance and humbly stand on some pretty big shoulders that, to the point of death, fell forward in their commitment and conviction for change. This is not a time to look back, but like the old spiritual sings, to "keep [our] hand on the plow, hold on, hold on."

Known as the "Gospel Plow (Hold On)," or "Keep Your Hand on the Plow," this African American spiritual is based on the words of Christ in Luke 9:62: "No one who puts a hand to the plow and looks back is fit for service in the kingdom of God."

This song was originally written in the early twentieth century and was later modified and sung as "Keep Your Eyes on the Prize." While there have been many lyrics rearranged and contemporized, especially during the civil rights movement, the message holds fast. We are doing the work of resistance; we need to keep moving forward and not let go of the plow—in so doing we will be fit for service in the kingdom of God.

> Heard the voice of Jesus say, come unto me, I am the way.
> Keep your hand on the plow, hold on.
> When my way gets dark as night, I know the Lord will be my light,
> Keep your hand on the plow, hold on.
> Hold on. Hold on. Keep your hand on the plow, hold on.[10]

We have determined to be forward-facing people who envision hope, see the reality of what is and the possibility of what can be. We plant our small, simple, yet steadfast efforts like a seed into the soil of a shared big, long work. We are not faint of heart, but full of faith. We do not shrink back; we are moving and growing forward, joining others, learning how to stay at the table for the long haul.

"HOLD ON"

youtube.com/watch?v=lX6oHKTomtM

THE COVENANT PRAYER

I am no longer my own, but yours.

Put me to what you will, place me with whom you will.

Put me to doing, put me to suffering.

Let me be put to work for you or set aside for you,

Praised for you or criticized for you.

Let me be full, let me be empty.

Let me have all things, let me have nothing.

I freely and fully surrender all things

To your glory and service.

And now, O wonderful and holy God,

Creator, Redeemer, and Sustainer,

You are mine, and I am yours.

So be it.

And the covenant, which I have made on earth,

Let it also be made in heaven.

Amen.[1]

STEPS INTO SERVING THE MOVEMENT

1. Do you have a walking-in story? If so, what are things that stretched you? What was different because of your walking in? Are there things you wish you had known earlier? Did you make any changes after that experience? If so, what were they?

2. If you have not begun to take steps in, how can you begin to do that?

3. What types of resistance toward injustice are you seeing? What issues move your heart for justice? Have you taken any first steps to participating in on-the-ground movement work? Why or why not? If yes, how did it go?

4. Have you reached out to leaders who are doing local work on issues that are important to you too? If not, begin to reach out. If yes, how did it go?

5. Choosing to be humble is an act of bravery. What ways has humility helped support efforts you are seeing and/or experiencing regarding justice in the church, in your community, in the country, or throughout the world?

6. Have you set up any one-on-one meetings or attended a local civic event where issues you care about are being represented? If yes, have you found groups that you can join? How do you hope to become involved? If not, how can you hold yourself accountable to these forward responses?

7. How have you seen people "fall forward" in their commitment toward justice and resistance work? What do you admire in them? What is distinct about their decisions? How can you fall forward in your context of serving the movement?

PART II

STAY AT
THE TABLE

4

THE LONG ARC

FOUR DAYS BEFORE HIS DEATH, Martin Luther King Jr. stood at the National Cathedral in Washington, DC, for the last time and said, "The arc of the moral universe is long but it bends toward justice."[1] It was a modification of a quote by the Reverend Theodore Parker, an abolitionist whose tireless effort to end slavery seemed close yet out of reach, who said: "I do not pretend to understand the moral universe; the arc is a long one, my eye reaches but little ways; I cannot calculate the curve and complete the figure by the experience of sight; I can divine it by conscience. And from what I see I am sure it bends toward justice."[2]

The work of kingdom justice, of joining Christ in his ongoing restoration of the world, is a long work; it is not subject to determined check lists, it does not run linear. The work to reverse systematic oppression needs people who are committed to staying when change looks like it is far from around the bend. When the marching has died down and many have gone home, this is the ongoing, necessary work of change. This work needs people who are not trying to jockey for position or place. This is the ongoing foundational work of learning, strategizing, and organizing to bring important issues to those who have the power to make change.

Throughout this book I refer to "the table." This is a metaphor I use to describe the collection of people working toward change. Sometimes there is a literal table that you are invited to; sometimes this metaphoric table begins as a one-on-one meeting at a coffee shop, or through building relationships with others at a local town hall, a small church basement gathering, or a Zoom room. Whatever the dynamic, small group or large organized entity, all of this is the table. When I say, "stay at the table," don't spend too much time worrying about what the table might look like or if you are sitting at it: The word I want you to focus on is the word *stay* because that is the discipline.

Redemption is on the rise, and as we stay faithful, we grow to see and believe that justice will come—we can see restoration before us. That is why at the table you will need to discipline yourself to stay. You will have to work with people who are different from you, who have different experiences, faith traditions (or no faith at all), and racial, political, sexual, and cultural perspectives. You will have to learn how to receive information that will feel unfamiliar, cause insecurities to rise, and at times feel extremely personal. Stay anyway.

You need to discern where you are going to plant some roots and, when the time reveals itself, where to invest your efforts with others. You will need to learn, to practice, and to choose repeatedly to stay. As you consider your next place of engagement, you need to first consider your cost.

CONSIDER THE COST

Jesus was a radical. Throughout his life and ministry, he boldly spoke against pompous religious leaders and the oppressive systems they perpetuated. He spoke up for the poor and the marginalized. Very practically and with compassion he kept healing and feeding people through miracles, further demonstrating his God power. All of this activity was drawing bigger and bigger crowds.

With such a powerful message that many were hungry for, he went from town to town and the numbers who followed him continued to grow. Beyond his disciples, he also had many committed followers and others who came to join the revolutionary party. Jesus had a lot of "groupies."

One day, when he was traveling, he turned to the throngs of people who were following him and said, "If anyone comes to me and does not hate father and mother, wife and children, brothers and sisters—yes, even their own life—such a person cannot be my disciple. And whoever does not carry their cross and follow me cannot be my disciple" (Luke 14:26-27).

Jesus knew that it would cost a lot from those who were following him and his message of the kingdom. He knew because it had cost *him* a lot. In addition to being driven out of the local synagogue for his message, his mother and brothers worried for his mental health and just wanted him to come home and live a normal, safe life (Mark 3:20-21). He knew that the voices closest to us are powerful motivators. I don't believe Jesus was calling people to literally hate their families—he was using strong words to illustrate the cost of leaving the familiar and acceptable status quo to speak into and practice living a life of the kingdom. He wanted to make sure that in the long work of following him, people realized that the cost of discipleship was significant and should be calculated.

Jesus also told this parable:

> Suppose one of you wants to build a tower. Won't you first sit down and estimate the cost to see if you have enough money to complete it? For if you lay the foundation and are not able to finish it, everyone who sees it will ridicule you, saying, "This person began to build and wasn't able to finish." . . . In the same way, those of you who do not give up everything you have cannot be my disciples. (Luke 14: 28-33)

The work of resistance, of justice, of restoration is not a fast work and it is a work that does not come cheap. Like the builder, you must consider what the sacrifices are going to look like. It's a privilege to sit at the table and serve where needed in an ongoing way; it is also a sacrifice. Furthermore, nobody there wants to hear how busy you are and the sacrifices it took for you to get there. Everyone is busy, everyone is sacrificing for this work— this is our gift to the movement. Consider your cost before you step in so that you can stay at work for the long haul.

THE LONG HAUL

One of the best, most amazing gifts I have received at the tables where I have served are relationships with like-minded people. Many of these community members, colleagues, and leaders have become some of my dearest mentors and friends. The work is long, and it was never meant to be done alone. Planting yourself for the journey and staying in it yield community and friendship that will shape and sustain you for the long haul.

One of those dearest relationships for me has been with my friend and mentor Rev. Dr. Alexia Salvatierra. We began to work together when my organizing work in Colorado needed to grow to include national support and strategy, and Alexia had the connections alongside decades of grassroots organizing to help support me and pave a way to make it happen. The two of us joined up, and once we started, we didn't stop. So many years together forming and re-forming tables for those who support immigration has resulted in a strong working and personal relationship. I am deeply grateful for her life and witness, and even more for her honesty, unrelenting passion for justice, commitment to the body of Christ, and how she looks for opportunities to support me personally.

Alexia is one of those people who considered the cost early in her spiritual formation and has lived her life working toward equity and justice. Most of her work has been in the faith space, but not limited only to faith communities nor her specific faith. She lives her life anchored in the good news of Christ and holds Christian orthodoxy and praxis with generosity. This openmindedness has been a foundation where so much good has been built, in her community, around the country, and globally.

During the 1970s, she came to know Christ through the Jesus movement. After that and before becoming an ordained congregational pastor in California, she worked as a missionary in the Philippines. There she served as a hospital chaplain, taught at St. Andrew's Episcopal Seminary, and ran a project working with the urban poor, training women to serve as chaplains to their neighbors.

In that season the country was going through a revolution known as the People Power Revolution. This country-wide revolution saw millions of Filipinos peacefully overthrow the dictator, President Ferdinand E. Marcos, in a fight to end his twenty-year regime and usher in a new democratic government. The Catholic church and other Christian faith traditions were a central part of that revolutionary leadership. Alexia was a part of the clergy arm of the pro-democracy movement during that time.

For the many hats Alexia has worn over her journey, her most well-defined and curated is as an organizer. Natural gifting and call, accompanied by local training early in her formation with national organizations, laid an important foundation. Later she was mentored by organizing giant of the civil rights movement, the Reverend James Lawson. Alexia is one of the country's top faith-rooted organizers—you can learn more about her faith-rooted organizing work and philosophy in her book, *Faith-Rooted Organizing: Mobilizing the Church in Service to the World.*

Alexia has walked the long road of justice and often shares the long timeline that reversing injustice will take. She faithfully reminds us to pay attention to what *has* been achieved and not only what is still before us, because the realities of sin are always present and at work in the world. Alexia's life and teaching encourage us to recognize that we have come so far, even as we wait for God to finish his work. Alexia did not show up with this wisdom—as it is for all of us, over the long haul, perspectives are shaped, tested, learned, and applied.

Shaping perspective for the long haul. While she was serving in the Philippines, Alexia had the opportunity to spend time with sugar plantation workers who had been trying to unionize themselves for fair wages and working conditions. Many of their families were malnourished because they were compensated so poorly. "An innovative young worker had initiated an act of creative resistance; to provide food for their children, she organized the women to plant banana trees around their huts."[3] Those who were managing the plantation were angry and sent guards to destroy the plants.

While the women were crying about this act of aggression, Alexia asked the woman who had organized the effort, "How can you continue in the face of such discouragement?" The woman simply assured Alexia that they would win.

Completely frustrated, Alexia challenged her, "When will you win?"

"Soon," said the organizer.

"Are you crazy?! What do you mean, soon?"

Her reply, "In the time of my daughter's daughter. Soon."[4]

Soon, but maybe not in our lifetime? People are dying in the streets and the fires of injustice are sweeping violently through now! "Maybe soon, maybe someday" does not feel like a satisfactory answer. We want justice now—people need justice now!

Preparing for the long haul. Alexia has often referenced the teaching of Reverend Lawson, who points to the story of Elijah and the prophets of Baal as an example of faithfully doing the work, waiting for God to move. The prophet Elijah challenged the prophets of Baal to prove that Yahweh was the one true God. The competing sides each built towers of wood, laid an animal sacrifice of a bull on the wood, and prayed that their deity would send fire from heaven to burn it up.

As recorded in 1 Kings 18, despite the prophets of Baal's dancing, praying, and wailing, their tower of wood and bull did not burn up. So, Elijah added a challenge to God, doused the sacrifice in water, and dug a trench and filled that with water. God's answer to Elijah's prayer? He rained fire from heaven and consumed everything, including the water!

What Lawson highlights in this story is that both groups had to do the work of getting the altars ready. Much of the long work is doing the daily altar-laying so that when the fires rain from heaven, we are ready to celebrate the good work that God is doing on behalf of his justice. Alexia encourages us to recognize that the long arc of the work does not have to discourage us. We can still rejoice in every step forward toward beloved community. We must see every immediate victory however, in the light of our ultimate goal. Reformation and revolution are ongoing processes, not events. Knowing that our goals will take generations to fully achieve necessitates a kind of faith and patience that is unfamiliar in a society addicted to instant reward.[5]

Setting expectations for the long haul. In the long work of resistance, it is important for us to wrap our minds around a lifetime of work for the long haul. I am an easily bored person—if I don't get results, I want to shift to something else—so I have had to learn a lot of discipline to be a part of the work of resistance. I have also learned that justice work is not on some to-do list, and it doesn't get done in a certain timeframe or according to my schedule. If I sincerely care about injustice, then I need to come to the table and learn how to sit at it no matter what.

The good news is, the long-haul work is shared. I love how activist Angela Davis speaks to the collective work and timeline: "I think the importance of doing activist work is precisely because it allows you to give back and to consider yourself not an individual who may have achieved whatever but to be a part of an ongoing historical movement."[6]

Building on the efforts that have been and are already in motion is exactly why you sit and stay at the table. Good work is happening. You can learn a lot from those who are sitting there. Yes, you will learn strategies and best practices, but one major piece that you will learn from others is how to stay and build into the collective, shared effort.

BUILDING TOGETHER

In 1962, Prathia Hall left her home in Philadelphia to join the voting rights efforts with SNCC in Georgia. She had grown up the daughter of a Baptist minister and became involved in civil rights work during college. Prathia was no stranger to protest, arrest, and physical attacks. She continued to stand strong in her faith and commitment to the work for civil rights.

Three days after being wounded by a segregationist's bullet, Prathia helped lead a prayer meeting in Terrell County, Georgia, on the site of Mount Olivet Baptist Church, recently burned to the ground by the KKK. The Reverend Dr. Martin Luther King Jr. was present for the prayer event, along with many other leaders in the movement.

They were gathering and praying earnestly, not as an activist tactic but as a way of life. Prathia led out in her prayer, saying over and over, "I have a dream," and then adding shared hopes of liberation.[7] Dr. King was so inspired that on the ride to the airport, he told Prathia he was so moved by her prayer of dreams that he wanted to use it.

Prathia Hall's prayer became Dr. King's prayer, and he used her inspired words to lead. One year later, on August 28, 1963, in front of the Lincoln Memorial in Washington, DC, Martin Luther King Jr. stood before a crowd of a quarter of a million people and gave his famous "I Have a Dream" speech.[8] I love how Senator Reverend Raphael Warnock referenced it in the PBS documentary *The Black Church*: "Before it was Martin's dream, it was Prathia's prayer."[9]

When sitting at the table, we learn that the work is collective and that it is shared. We need to inspire and be inspired, and the result of that inspiration is a shared celebration.

I have seen egos get in the way; I have fought to make sure at times that the ego isn't mine. The pressure is intense, so much is on the line—it's hard. But building a collective kingdom work is not about making superstars. The world wants a champion, but in the work of resistance we need to fight back against that pressure and ensure that we are sowing a *harvest* of champions to lead a collective movement for justice.

SAYING YES

It was July 2019 when I saw my friend's Facebook post: a young Nicaraguan man, the son of Assemblies of God pastors, had just been released from detention and needed a place to stay. He had been in detention for over five months after swimming across the Rio Grande River between Mexico and Texas and requesting asylum. He was twenty-one. I was drawn to what little I knew of him and his need, and went to talk to my husband immediately.

David and I have lived in an immigrant neighborhood for over twenty-five years. We are surrounded by people just like this young man. At that time, it was extremely common to share stories of desperation and need on a weekly basis with others who were coming from Central America to escape political and religious persecution. I did not need Facebook to tell me another story, because I had a front row seat to the pain and struggles of immigrants fleeing injustice. Something compelled me, however, to consider offering him a place to stay with us.

The timing could not have been more inconvenient. I was a couple of weeks from jumping into the US Senate race in the 2020 election.

Running for office in a state with over 104,000 square miles was going to be an all-consuming effort. I did not need any distractions, but I could not let this young man's situation go. As I stood there talking with my husband about helping I know I sounded desperate. We were standing at the bathroom counter, and when I stopped talking David turned, looked at me, and asked, "Michelle, do *you* want to do this? Do you really want to do this?" Knowing how much the commitment of taking someone in who needed a lot of legal, language, and life support was, I felt a desperate *Yes, I want to do this* release from my heart.

Within two days, Gixson was in our home. He spoke no English, had no money, no connections, no job. He had suffered so much before he got to our border to ask for help, yet with no regard for his personhood he had been treated inhumanely and unjustly when he asked for asylum, the legal way forward for him. He left the detention center after five and a half months of being treated like a criminal and with a $35,000 bond debt to a private prison industry. No one was assigned to give him the support he would need on this side of his journey, working to heal and move past the reason he had to leave his entire life in Nicaragua.

FOR JUSTICE, FOR PEACE

Gixson and his older brother Mixson were students at the University of Nicaragua. Gixson, whose parents had sacrificed much to afford them both an education, had worked hard to attend and pay for university. He was studying industrial engineering and working with a rural farming co-op to optimize farmers' agricultural goods, productions, and sales. The middle son of five, whose parents were farmers, tailors, and tent-making church planters, he loved his life and saw a strong future for himself doing good work for his community.

During this season, a local, municipal election took place. Corruption in national elections to small town and village positions was commonplace. Gixson and his brother Mixson, to support a more just, democratic election system, worked to expose the corruption. This effort cost Mixson his life.

Nicaragua is the poorest country in Central America and the second poorest in the Western Hemisphere. It is not a free country with fair and free elections, nor is freedom of speech protected. People who advocate for change, while living under a dictatorship that cares little about people's flourishing, are demonstrating immense bravery.

A couple of months after Mixson's death, students from the University of Nicaragua organized protests in the capital city of Managua and throughout the country to decry social security reforms, which raised taxes and decreased benefits. It became international news.[10] Gixson and his community participated in the protests in his area, using the opportunity to speak against the current dictator and further expose the murder of his brother.

These nationwide events set off a chain of activism that is still making impacts to this day: speaking against corrupt, oppressive leadership and demanding change. For Gixson, because of his boldness, he became a target of the government. By bravely sharing what had happened to his brother, he put his life in danger. Therefore, he could not stay. Pulling together whatever resources his family could afford, he left his family, his community, and his country. The sacrifice of leaving and possibly never seeing his family and country again became the only way forward. Twenty-eight days later, after a harrowing journey, he arrived at the United States, requested asylum, and was incarcerated for five and a half months. Days after his release, he moved in with us.

While Gixson's heart was with his family, his country, and his culture, he knew God was directing him toward a different way to support them. He specifically requested to live in a home where he could learn English; he understood he needed new skills for life in a new place. His roots had been planted so deeply in his family, culture, and country that there was no risk of becoming a different person—he knew who he was, what his community needed, and to this day remains focused on providing support to other asylum seekers and Nicaraguan community projects in his hometown. At times the waves of sadness for all he has lost hit him, but it has never caused him to give up or become deterred. Now fully bilingual and biliterate, gainfully employed, and a culturally adept man, he continues to plant new roots for life in a new place, supporting those from home, with a future he could not have anticipated.

SEEK THE PEACE

The prophet Jeremiah is often referred to as "the weeping prophet," prophesying at a time of impending doom: Judah was going into captivity, all the warnings were over. Israel, from the plentiful time of David and Solomon, had finally come to an end. Split kingdoms, battles won and lost, people's hearts back-and-forth to God, it was over—God's judgment was here. Living captive lives was now going to be reality. Jeremiah's was the final warning of truth and the people of God hated him for it. Jeremiah was a big downer at dinner tables and wouldn't let it rest. What bad, sad news he always had. Jeremiah faithfully carried the truth of God to hostile ears *and* had to live through the results of being overtaken and losing his home country too!

Jeremiah's words were powerful and Spirit-led and filled, but at the end of the day, Jeremiah was a human who was afraid and wanted to quit. Sometimes I am afraid and I want to quit too; in my humanity I want to sit in a corner and cry. I want to give up and allow my exhaustion to take over and to permit me to stop and no longer care. *I see the cost ahead and it's been so expensive already, isn't it time to be done?*

One day when I didn't think I could continue because of my great sadness, I decided I should get to know the weeping prophet a little better. He had a deep reason to cry—his people had walked away from God. Other prophets of the day were telling the leaders and people that judgment was not going to come and to not worry.

This is what I learned: Jeremiah's calling on his life came before his birth. God had appointed him to live in this moment in history for this prophetic work to the nations. Jeremiah, upon hearing God's word for him to share, did what any normal human would do—he argued and did not believe. Excuses began to flow. Excuses like being too young, not knowing how. He was feeling inadequate (Jeremiah 1:4-10). Today we would put it under the banner of imposter syndrome.

God responded:

Get yourself ready! Stand up and say to them whatever I command you. Do not be terrified by them, or I will terrify you before them. Today I have made you a fortified city, an iron pillar and a bronze wall to stand against the whole land—against the kings of Judah, its officials, its priests and the people of the land. They will fight against you but will not overcome you, for I am with you and will rescue you. (Jeremiah 1:17-19)

And from that point Jeremiah went, sad and afraid in his own humanity, but strong and protected in the strength of God.

Jeremiah told the people of God that because they turned from God, because of their unfaithfulness, disaster would come. He told them that they and their leaders were wicked and had grown fat and deceitful; they were rich and powerful, and their evil deeds had no limit. He told them they had no care for the orphans or offering of defense for the poor. This was everything God hated, and they knew it! Jeremiah was exposing not only the collective sin of a people but the evil hearts of them and their leaders. They were going down, and Jeremiah was not holding anything back.

When you bring it to today, I can imagine the lack of seriousness with which the people took the words of Jeremiah. Who was he anyway? They had other prophets who filled them with what they wanted to hear. The New Testament refers to it as itching ears (2 Timothy 4:3). Nothing is new under the sun, my friends. We resist the truth of God and daily exchange it for a lie; we are fine, we don't need to care beyond our own self interests. God understands and the status quo is A-okay.

The leaders and people of Jeremiah's day are not much different from those of today. Our humanity is common and our apathy for justice is the same. We tend to play it safe and assume that things will work out for us. We figure God is not serious about caring for the rights of the oppressed or joining them in their suffering. But in Jeremiah 5, the Lord says, "A horrible and shocking thing has happened in the land: The prophets prophesy lies, the priests rule by their own authority, and my people love it this way. But what will you do in the end?" (vv. 30-31).

And today? The church's leaders have become distracted. They do not take God's call and law seriously. They have determined the measuring line for justice and the response by the church. They love it. But what are we going to do in the end? It doesn't seem too shocking to me, but it is horrible.

Jeremiah remained a constant voice through the consequences. For forty years he faithfully showed up to speak the truth. Talk about a long haul! He didn't stand on the outskirts yelling, "You deserved this. I told you so." No, he walked people through the pain of the consequences. He helped them set a vision of a long life in a foreign place. In Jeremiah 29, he writes a letter of instruction and hope to the exiles. He tells them that even in the midst of living in exile, they shouldn't be so future-minded about what *will* happen—restoration—but instead dig roots and invest in the now.

That seems strange considering resistance work too. I want to show up to change injustice *now* and see it change quickly. I don't want to experience the downward mobility, the rejection, the loss, the poverty, or the poor-in-spirit state of those who are oppressed. Gixson and others are a great example of unexplainable courage, tremendous faithfulness to thrive where God places them, and adaptability to grow in unfamiliar and unperceived ways.

We must be willing to sit and serve for the long haul. Not as a stranger for a season, but as a neighbor and way of life. Understand that in sitting at the table you are purposing to seek peace and welfare by investing in your community. Seek the prosperity of the movement, not as a greedy grabber but as one who is sowing into the work, and reap community and solidarity. The Lord said to those in exile: "Seek the peace and prosperity of the city to which I have carried you into exile. Pray to the LORD for it, because if it prospers, you too will prosper" (Jeremiah 29:7).

The parallel for the message of this chapter is this: don't be in such a rush to get in and out. Don't believe the lie that if just one thing changes, it will all work out and you are free to go back and live your life for yourself. The layers of structural injustice demand more than one act, even if that action is significant. This is a lifestyle for the long haul. This is the long work of justice, the long work of the kingdom, so invest in the people, the culture, and a new way of living.

WE SHALL OVERCOME, SOMEDAY

Regardless of our starting and ending point, God is doing the work. We work in collaboration with people who bring to the moment a deposit into the greater movement of justice. We see this kind of "baton passing" all throughout Scripture: Moses passing the mantle to Joshua to bring the people into the Promised Land (Numbers 27:22-23); the prophets carrying the word of the Lord to a rebellious people generation after generation; John the Baptist telling the people that he is merely the one paving the way for Jesus (Luke 3:16); Paul planting so Apollos can water (1 Corinthians 3:6-8). In these stories and others, God is the One who makes it grow and produce—we are a part of a long-standing, faith-rooted-effort relay, investing across generations in the kingdom.

Representative John Lewis passed away in July of 2020. A giant for civil rights who served in the House of Representatives from 1987 until his death, he did not get his passion for justice in Washington, DC. As the chairman of the SNCC during the height of the civil rights movement in the 1960s, he led voter registration drives, integrated the South, and was one of the six key leaders who organized and led the March on Washington in 1963, among other things.

His activism is one of legends and the movement for racial justice in the United States would not have been what it was had not Representative Lewis been present. Known for a great many

moving words backed up with faith in action, this quote from
June 2018 became personally inspiring during a challenging
season: "Do not get lost in a sea of despair. Be hopeful, be opti-
mistic. Our struggle is not the struggle of a day, a week, a month,
or a year, it is the struggle of a lifetime. Never, ever be afraid to
make some noise and get in good trouble, necessary trouble."[11]

The song "We Shall Overcome" was a strength to John Lewis
in his "struggle of a lifetime."

> In his book *Walking with the Wind: A Memoir of the Movement*,
> he tells of joining the civil rights cause as a teenager off the
> farm in Alabama. He became a leader. He was jailed; he was
> beaten. His skull was fractured in Selma on the day that was
> called Bloody Sunday. He shared that the song, "We Shall
> Overcome" sustained him throughout the years of struggle—
> especially those moments when demonstrators who had
> been beaten, arrested or detained would stand and sing it
> together. "It gave you a sense of faith, a sense of strength,
> to continue to struggle, to continue to push on. And you
> would lose your sense of fear," Lewis says. "You were pre-
> pared to march into hell's fire."[12]

"We Shall Overcome" became the anthem of the civil rights
movement. A song that was being sung together in the streets, by
those marching for civil rights across the country. It crossed ages,
cultures, races, and eventually continents.

It was performed to a nationally televised audience at the
March on Washington, August 1963, by folk singer-songwriter
Joan Baez. At the age of twenty-two, with her guitar she led over
three hundred thousand people in the powerful lyrics. That song
and its message did not begin with Joan or other young White

musicians and activists like Bob Dylan or Pete Seeger. Their national platforms and singing and marching hand in hand with Black civil rights activists of the day lifted the message of the song, along with its hopes of a brighter future, so that it is well-known throughout the world today.

The origins of the song show the legacy of shared work. A partial melody from the Catholic hymn "O Sanctissima," composed in 1790, was threaded together with songs that were sung by slaves in the United States, "I'll Be All Right" and "No More Auction Block for Me." It later became linked to a hymn written after 1900 titled "I'll Overcome Someday." That hymn was written by the Reverend Dr. Charles Tindley, a Black Methodist pastor.

The song's lyrics changed from "I'll Overcome" to "We'll Overcome"

> during a 1945–1946 labor strike against American Tobacco in Charleston, South Carolina. African American women strikers, seeking a pay raise to 30 cents an hour, sang as they picketed. "I Will Overcome" was a favorite song of Lucille Simmons, one of the strikers. But she gave the song a powerful sense of solidarity by changing the "I" into "We" as they sang together.[13]

By 1947, Simmons brought the song to Highlander Folk School where the head of the school's cultural program, Zilphia Horton, shared it with others and specifically Pete Seeger.[14] Seeger changed the words "We will" to the words "We shall," inspiring a new generation to work together for shared liberation.

If we are to overcome someday, we need to believe deeply in our hearts. We need to work hand in hand, not in competition but in collaboration, so that one day we can be at peace and live free.

We shall overcome,
We shall overcome,
We shall overcome, some day.
Oh, deep in my heart, I do believe
We shall overcome, some day.
We'll walk hand in hand . . .
We shall live in peace . . .
We shall all be free . . .
We are not afraid . . .
We shall overcome . . .
Oh, deep in my heart,
I do believe
We shall overcome, some day.[15]

"WE SHALL OVERCOME"

youtube.com/watch?v=2WO2hDYBcqU

5

RESILIENCE

It was early winter 2021, and people were beginning to feel comfortable meeting up and sharing in-person space after so many months in pandemic isolation. I headed over to the ministry a longtime friend was leading. An African American woman, mother of sons, and a pastor, she is one of the most resilient, brave people I am honored to call my sister. After our initial greetings, we settled down for a long-awaited conversation; the past year had held so much dynamic change.

"Michelle," she said, "I am down to four White friends who I can trust. If you and [she named the three other friends] decide to pack it in and no longer walk this walk, I am done too."

So much held in that sentence—there was sadness that the circle of trust was so small, grief that so few people were committed to working together in the same long-haul resistance work for just systems, and there was exhaustion. Exhaustion in continuing to work in an unreconciled church that was complicit in racism and deeply offended when it was revealed.

I had no response to her initially, feeling the weight of it all. After I listened and before the conversation ended, I said, "I am not going anywhere."

The relational stakes are high for everyone in the work. Believing and understanding we are not alone is elemental. Our friends in the movement are tired and need to know that regardless of skin tone, struggle, and slow change, we are committed and they aren't alone. Solidarity in the struggle keeps us going, solidarity on every side.

It becomes even more challenging when those we are sitting with don't look like us or share similar cultural norms or ethos. We have come together on behalf of a shared hope, but the roads that brought us together are vastly different. Oftentimes those paths are riddled with conflict, hurt, and betrayal, and having us there can expose past trauma. We may have had nothing to do with the individual or specific trauma, but that does not mean we don't represent it. Getting to the shared place of working and staying together isn't always comfortable. It is stretching work for people on every side, which can get very personal at times, requiring new growth and new faith.

GETTING PERSONAL

The summer of 2016 was a hot mess. In July before the presidential election, I found myself sitting in a group of justice advocates at North Park Seminary in Chicago, Illinois. There were about sixty advocates sitting in the room at the time; we were all self-described evangelicals, nearly all were leaders of color. All of us were in debate on the church, evangelicals, and the upcoming Trump versus Clinton election.

Many in the group did not know each other. Trust existed between the leadership, but the rest of us were starting from the ground up. The central theme of the time, whether on the agenda or not, was the anger and disgust at White evangelicals specifically. I sat there as one of the few Whites in the room. Several people did not know me, they did not know my work, they did not care, and they had no issue sharing their disgust and disdain for my kind. Their anger, which was directed to White evangelicals, began to be directed at me.

"Why are you even here?" one woman asked with disgust. She related horrible experiences she had encountered from White evangelical women trying to solicit her name and leadership for book endorsements and social media connections. She specifically called out how White women had requested to be her Facebook friend. She looked at me and said, "We are not friends. Don't ask me to be your Facebook friend."

I sat quietly looking at her and listening. I did not look away or down. I took in her pain as the token stereotypical White woman. I actually felt it, not the need to defend against it or add to her diatribe, but I took it in. The moment was really hard, and I worked hard to not make it personal even as I tried to feel it personally. It felt so vulnerable.

Here's the reality—everyone is vulnerable. Opening spaces to include those who represent the oppressor in an environment takes courage, because everyone needs safe spaces. Sitting there with my White skin did not represent safe. I did however represent myself, and regardless of what had taken place this was her day, and I wasn't about to add to the pain of her experiences.

After the session ended, people whose friendships we had in common rushed to explain away what she had said, trying to take away the sting. I listened to them without response. They were trying to smooth things over, but the reality was, this was the real pain of this woman of color, and White women had done a lot of harm to her. Regardless of whether I did the harm directly, I represented harm, and in that setting she wanted to share her truest, rawest feelings.

That day was the first of many days where she and I would share space. During that gathering, I did not try to get to know her or try to defend why I was different. I also did not hold anger or defense in my heart. This is a reality of the work—it's real racial dynamics that we cannot shy away from or take personally unless we did do something and need to apologize and make it right. In this kind of situation all we can do is work to create a new story and build our reputation as someone who is listening, humble, and open, and that takes time.

I have never asked her about that day so long ago. In some ways it felt like an initiation; in other ways I understood that she had to test what or who is safe. Eventually she came to understand and respect my place at the table as one of service to the movement. I was not going to be one of those people to hijack her voice, her platform, or her name to bolster my own. I would become known as someone who wanted to join in and lift the voices closest to the pain, defer to directly impacted leadership, and do whatever I could to make sure the movement was lifted higher and forward.

After our first shared experience, I arrived home and turned on my computer to get some work done. I looked at my Facebook notifications, and there sat a friend request from her. I smiled with gratitude at this small but meaningful gesture. This would begin a new day forward where we would continue to cross paths and steward future shared efforts for a more just and peaceful world.

No one is handed resilience. Whether from personal or collective tragedy, humanity needs to get back up from hardship and move forward. Resilience is not something we are born with; it is something we earn that makes us adaptable, stretchy, and able to return. We cannot give our resilience to others, but we can practice and build it together. The more we practice getting back up, the more we grow.

In this work there is little use for inflexible, rigid, or stiff people. Those kinds of people get pushed down, break, and quit. Pray for resilience. Pray for forbearance. Praise that those who have gone before have taught us the way forward.

HOSEA

The prophet Hosea was defined by resilience. Hosea's life story gives evidence of someone persisting in the face of extreme adversity, and demonstrates the faithful, unrelenting compassion and forgiveness of God for his people.

Hosea was one of the earliest of the prophets. His voice and service came about after the northern and southern kingdoms split. He was in the northern part of the kingdom of Israel, during the reign of Jeroboam II, who was one of the evilest kings of Israel. Hosea prophesied about the ways of God, the rebellion of his people, and the need to return to God, who offers restoration.

God used Hosea's life as an allegory demonstrating the relationship between God and his people Israel. Hosea's life shows two major takeaways: stay committed to God's plan for your life, and God's love is a covenant bond that never breaks regardless of our actions.

The Lord tells Hosea: "'Go, marry a promiscuous woman and have children with her, for like an adulterous wife this land is guilty of unfaithfulness to the LORD.' So he married Gomer daughter of Diblaim, and she conceived and bore him a son" (Hosea 1:2-3).

Gomer went on to give him another son and daughter. They were all given prophetic names: Their first son was named Jezreel because of future punishment God would inflict on the kingdom of Israel. The other two were called Lo-Ruhamah, which means "not loved," and Lo-Ammi, which means "not my people." Hosea is often referred to as the prophet of doom, not just because of the future doom destined for the people of Israel, but also because of the living legacy of his family and what they signified.

Hosea's marriage was a disaster. Because he married an unfaithful woman, it did not take long before she left Hosea to live with another man, and Hosea had to go find her and pay money to get her back. Hosea tells her that she needs to live a life of fidelity to him and reaffirms that he will do the same by staying faithful to her.

We don't know what happened to Hosea or Gomer after that, but the illustration that God demonstrates through their marriage is a one-sided passion and love. The people of Israel were fine when they had God, but they shared their hearts with worship to Baal. They were faithless, but because of the covenant God made with them, God would never ultimately separate himself from them. He always allowed restoration to be a part of the future story:

> Come, let us return to the LORD. He has torn us to pieces but he will heal us; he has injured us but he will bind up our wounds. . . . Let us acknowledge the LORD; let us press on to acknowledge him. As surely as the sun rises, he will

appear; he will come to us like the winter rains, like the spring rains that water the earth. (Hosea 6:1-3)

Despite the turning of the people of Israel, God remained faithful, had compassion, and did not destroy them. "I will not carry out my fierce anger, nor will I devastate Ephraim again. For I am God, and not a man—the Holy One among you. I will not come against their cities" (Hosea 11:9).

Hosea and Gomer's marriage was a literal demonstration of the unfaithfulness of people to the justice and heart of God, as well as the commitment of covenant love that God will restore. We are human beings, unable to restore. But God is persistent, and his love is adaptable to our shifts; his grace meets us where we are at. Resilience may not be something we are born with, but we can learn resilience through a submitted life of service to God because he shows himself faithful.

The work of resistance is supernatural and needs a supernatural response, the Spirit alive in us. We must remain committed to living a life connected to the values and heart of God and call on him in prayer knowing that he will hear and respond quickly. He is always at work for the restoration of individual, societal, and structural brokenness—it is the work of Christ and his justice.

PERSISTENT PRAYER

The practice of spiritual disciplines is foundational to any work of the Spirit. As doers of justice, we are literally in a wrestle against powers and forces of evil, disguised as people and with strongholds in systems. Staying faithful and holding an open posture toward shared transformation and change takes discipline. As the elders who have gone before have demonstrated time and again, prayer is an essential spiritual practice in the work of resistance.

Sometimes that prayer is done as a public witness. I have held countless prayer meetings on the steps of public buildings, at places of worship, and in community locations where tragedies occurred. Once I was arrested while publicly praying in front of the Speaker of the House's office in support of Dreamers (I was arrested for blocking the door). We pray because we know that God is listening. We pray publicly to let others know we believe that God is our higher power, calling us to work together toward his justice. Prayer is not a tactic of activism but an ongoing way of life. We pray individually, corporately, and publicly because we know the God of justice, who hears and will respond.

I love how activist and author Donna Barber speaks to prayer regarding our often "action junkie" lifestyle of activism. Prayer seems to be the last thing we want to slow down to do:

> We meet and we march. We shout and we seethe. Then at the end of long and frustrating days, we fall into bed exhausted. . . . And every now and then, perhaps through half-open, tired eyes, we pray. . . . [It's hard] slowing down, standing still, taking a moment to sit in the pause, and breathe. . . . When we pray, we again acknowledge that justice is not only our work but also the identity and plan of a just God being revealed in the earth. Power is released. Resources are given. Doors, windows, and hearts are opened. Minds, laws, and sometimes even the course of nature, change.[1]

Jesus wanted his disciples to understand the power of persistent prayer and the heart of the Father who was listening to their prayers. To help them understand, he shared this parable of the persistent widow:

In a certain town there was a judge who neither feared God
nor cared what people thought. And there was a widow in
that town who kept coming to him with the plea, "Grant me
justice against my adversary." For some time he refused. But
finally he said to himself, "Even though I don't fear God or
care what people think, yet because this widow keeps both-
ering me, I will see that she gets justice, so that she won't
eventually come and attack me!" (Luke 18:2-5)

This judge who did not care gave in because he could not be
bothered. He knew that the widow was persistent and was not
going to stop until she got what she needed. Sometimes we need
to be resilient and unwavering, simply because in doing so we
wear people down and they finally give in!

For many years I pulled faith leaders together to meet with
then representative Mike Coffman's office to support just immigration reform legislation. Coffman's predecessor had been most
known for speaking against immigration reform, even speaking
against his party leader's comprehensive immigration proposal.

Rep. Coffman was new and had bought a lot of the immigration
hardliners of his predecessor. I remember our first meeting with
the new congressman. During that first meeting, he would not
hear us. He didn't care about our presentation speaking to personal faith, which he also shared. He was not interested in our
statistics or our stories. We got nowhere.

We left, frustrated but committed. So committed that as we
closed up the meeting, I said we would be back. I told him we were
building a coalition of faith leaders, and though the list might be
small now, we would be growing.

And grow and return we did. Over and over in his DC and district offices we brought new leaders, stories, pictures, immigrants.

We also prayed. Sometimes we prayed outside his office when we did not have a meeting. We even bought a billboard in his district on a major thoroughfare by his office.

The week the billboard was erected, a group of district pastors and leaders met up at the billboard to pray. We prayed for immigrants, we prayed for just immigration reform. We prayed for Rep. Coffman's heart to open in new ways and to join us in our quest for justice for immigrants. That prayer meeting was in the heat of the summer, in a parking lot outside a local sexually-oriented building, and we invited the media—as anyone who is working to move their personal convictions to a public place would. We were praying publicly and testifying to what we wanted to see, under a sign with the bold green letters "Congress we are praying for you!" All the while having those prayers reported in the local news.

A year later, we saw Rep. Coffman part with his caucus in a very bold way. This is an unprecedented practice in elected officials because party loyalties are held steadfast. He penned an op-ed in *The Denver Post* declaring the need for comprehensive immigration reform.[2] He changed! He became someone who worked across the aisle, standing alone among his closest colleagues in his conviction that immigration reform was the only way forward.

I remember reading an *LA Times* article a couple of weeks after this all took place. Giving reason for his change, it read, "During the Senate debate this spring, Coffman's Colorado office was deluged with calls and petitions," quoting Dustin Zvonek, his district director. "Ten days in a row, evangelical churchgoers held prayer vigils in the office."[3]

I wish I could share that immigration reform happened because of our and Rep. Coffman's efforts at that time, but complete overhaul in a divisive policy remained unchanged. However, cracks of light in the darkness of injustice appeared, and the inability to see was changed. We saw evidence that persistence and prayer could make a change.

I remember, about a year later, sitting next to Rep. Coffman at a breakfast with local pastors to talk about immigration reform once again. I asked him quite candidly how to get his other Republican Colorado colleagues to share his perspective. He responded quite simply, "Keep doing what you did with me; keep going. Keep telling and sharing your stories. They will change."

The deeper message of the parable of the persistent widow goes beyond wearing someone down, but it is about remaining persistent in prayer. When we pray to the One who established justice, he cares and is always working to bring about justice. We who cry out to him day and night, believing that he will respond quickly, need to continue in deep faith. Jesus reminds us that there is incredible faith needed to keep a lifestyle of persistent prayer.

> And the Lord said, "Listen to what the unjust judge says. And will not God bring about justice for his chosen ones, who cry out to him day and night? Will he keep putting them off? I tell you, he will see that they get justice, and quickly. However, when the Son of Man comes, will he find faith on the earth?" (Luke 18:6-8)

The challenge before us is this: Will we pray with such faith? Will we not quit when we don't see quick evidence of what we are praying for? When all is done and Jesus returns, will he find this kind of radical, resilient faith on the earth?

BEYOND THOUGHTS AND PRAYERS

Reverend Traci Blackmon was a nurse-turned-preacher in Ferguson, Missouri. Faithfully, she walked alongside her community, baptizing, burying, counseling, and comforting. In August 2013, Rev. Blackmon oversaw a funeral for a twenty-one-year-old woman who was killed in a drive-by shooting in St. Louis. At the funeral, a young woman was so moved by Blackmon's leadership that she took her business card.

One year later, in the Canfield Green apartments where that young woman lived, her family was returning to their home and passed Michael Brown Jr.'s dead body. Needing a pastor, she found the business card and called Blackmon.

Blackmon responded that night and walked alongside her community to help them bury the young man. She also took to the streets for change. She was an important, unifying pastoral voice of truth in Ferguson over the coming months:

> We have to reclaim the language of faith. We have to stop defining ourselves by those who are misappropriating faith. We have to be more vocal about who we are, and what we stand for. . . . So I am not "Religious Left," I'm not "Religious Right"—I'm a disciple of Jesus Christ. I'm not preaching a progressive gospel, I'm not preaching a Social Gospel—I'm preaching *the* Gospel.[4]

Blackmon's community leadership and organizing are centered around prayer. She was inspired by this direct action of prayer from abolitionist and former slave Frederick Douglass, who said, "Praying for freedom never did me any good till I started praying with my feet." She goes on to say:

> It's time for us to stop waiting on the Lord to do everything and understand that we are the embodiment of Christ on

this earth, and we have to, not just pray with our mouths, but pray with our actions. It means we need to be on the ground. It means we need to be ministering to those people who are hurting. We need to stop waiting for people to come into our sanctuaries; we need to go out into the streets.[5]

Rev. Blackmon embodies what it means to be full of faith and resilient. In the midst of so much difficulty, she did not break but adapted. She took her pastoral care, her commitment to prayer, to the streets, and to this day continues to lead in the work of racial justice.

I recently had the opportunity to speak with Rev. Blackmon about her faith-rooted activism journey. Much like so many leaders of faith before her, she shared,

I wasn't trying to do activism. I came because I heard the cries of someone. During the Ferguson days people from all across the country were coming to our community. One of the litmus tests became this question: "When did you join the front lines?"

People would share, "I came to the front lines on day . . . one, two, seven." That question was a social baptism of fire. You don't *go* to a front line, but a lived ministry *brings* a front line to you. Activism is not defined by action in the streets but in places like dinner tables, hospital rooms, in places where cameras are not watching.[6]

PRAYING AND PRACTICING UNITY

One of the most powerful and beautiful resources in the work of resistance is in coming together across racial, political, socioeconomic spectrums, united under one banner. We have seen it happen in a flash, like when Republicans and Democrats sang an impromptu rendition of "God Bless America" together after the 9/11 attacks.[7] Sadly, this kind of unity is rare, and we too often resist putting into practice what is needed to make it happen.

I have always deeply admired the leadership of my elder and mentor Dr. Barbara Williams-Skinner, a revered African American lawyer who became the first female executive director of the Congressional Black Caucus.[8] She began her career in the halls of power in Washington, DC, and at that time came to a deep understanding of who Christ is. She began to lead in ways that were completely contrary to the polarizing culture of national politics and power. Knowing that building bridges across political parties was going to be huge Spirit work, she moved her personal prayers to a public and disciplined place.

For the National Prayer Breakfast in 1981, she was asked to pray before four thousand people for President Ronald Reagan. Her immediate response was, "Absolutely not!" But after a softening of her heart, she began to ask God how to pray for someone she disliked so much. With only a week before the breakfast she told God, "God, I'm not sure what's going on here, but you're going to be embarrassed because I do not know what to pray for a Republican president who hates poor people."[9]

The day arrived and she still had nothing. Arriving at the room, she watched as President Reagan and First Lady Nancy entered the room. Something transformative happened to her as she saw them—she did not see him as a president who held different political opinions but as a man and his wife. They were mere humans who needed restoration and help just like anyone else. In recognizing his humanity, she was able to pray true prayers for him. Later she reflected, "I don't know if God changed Ronald Reagan but he did change me. I surrendered myself to pray the prayer God had for me."[10]

Several years later she was able to reach out across the table and hold President Obama's hands in prayer, seeing his humanity and understanding the Spirit power he needed to lead, from husband and father to leader of the free world. President Trump would test her commitment in new ways to pray for leaders whether we agree with them or not. "God's word calls believers to pray for those in leadership despite their political persuasion, that their decisions will line up with God's word. Our primary loyalty is to God."[11]

SEEDS OF HOPE

Nearly every gathering of faith-rooted justice leaders I have attended takes time out to address how to feed our souls for the long journey. I love the opportunity to listen to what ministers to people and keeps them going. Prayer, reading Scripture, singing songs are often at the top of the list. No one thing works for each person, and I have had to change up my practices over the years. My life, schedule, and work are in perpetual motion, so I need to be flexible on how to stay disciplined. I have also added two less common spiritual disciplines: walking and gardening.

When the Covid-19 pandemic isolation came, like everyone else I moved to exclusively remote work. I am an active person who loves people. As an off-the-chart extrovert, I thrived for several years in my job where I was able to be in a different city a few weeks a month. I stayed connected to my team through online platforms but rarely had to sit behind a computer for days straight.

Now, day after day sitting behind a computer doing work on video was slowing killing me. Work travel all but disappeared, and from that point forward I found myself in a physical space that was draining. I needed to learn a new kind of resilience. Once we were able to get out and about again, my work continued to remain online and there would be days on end that I would have no reason to leave my house. I had to get out.

Colorado winters are unpredictable. You can have a sunny sixty-degree day in January or a three-foot blizzard in March. I was determined to not allow weather to impact my need to get outside. I committed to walk every day and three days a week to walk over four miles. That time to clear my head, look at the scenery, listen to my surroundings, talk with family, friends, and colleagues became such a cherished new practice. It fed my soul deeply.

Gardening has always been a hobby-turned-spiritual-practice for me.[12] I need to watch life grow. Years ago when I moved to Denver, outside the community house's back door there was a small patch of dirt next to the alley—about three square feet. One day as I was at my local Walgreens I saw seed packets marked 10 for $1. I was drawn to them, despite there being only two options—dill and lettuce. I didn't care. I was ready to try something new and get my hands dirty.

Turning over the dirt I found an initial harvest of broken glass, random parts, and pantyhose. Regardless, I planted with excitement and waited for things to grow. When they actually did, I was hooked.

As years went by my annual efforts grew more consistent and elaborate, moving beyond seeds from Walgreens to actual garden centers. To this day I walk adoringly through the aisles of blooming flowers and plants. Wondering why I work to grow plants from tiny, finicky seeds? Who has time to plant seeds indoors, months in advance, and nurture their growth? It would be so much easier to buy mature plants, right?

It's true; there are more efficient ways to have a garden than starting from seeds. At times I wish I could succumb, but the gardener and the activist inside me hold back. I have become enthralled with the process of watching something grow from its beginning.

Ironically, seeds do not look like they will grow into anything needed or beautiful. They look like something you would sweep into a dustpan and discard. Yet, the sheer act of placing them in dirt, believing they will grow, points directly to a crucial element needed in our work: hope.

Hope enables you to believe and act, regardless of what you see. Faith, hope's twin, is intrinsically linked. Both require you to believe in the unseen and set a vision of what can be. It's a moving forward, not because the results are guaranteed, but because you believe they are worth walking toward.

Hebrews 11, often referred to as the "By Faith" chapter, lists the matriarchs and patriarchs of the Bible who chose to walk by faith toward a vision of what could be without its evidence. In Hebrews 11:13 we see these people of faith, resilient in their hoping until their deaths. They "welcomed [what they hoped for] from a distance," having a vision of what could be.

As faith-rooted activists, we can find ourselves wondering if the seeds we plant will ever poke their heads out of the ground. How long must we wait? Will we have to replant? Will we ever see evidence of our efforts? Much of my activist life is spent planting seeds without much evidence of growth, placing hopes and ideals into proverbial dirt, waiting for fruit. I have learned through activism and gardening's intersection the following correlations. We need the following:

- *Timing*—Timing is essential. Nothing is done on a whim. It takes time for seedling plants to transition from a controlled environment to unpredictable elements. Regardless of what is cultivated independently, the time to stand up for community is not randomly chosen but carefully considered and approached sustainably.

- *Foundation*—The strength of roots depends on the quality of the soil. Jesus talks about the importance of soil enabling seeds to take root. In activism, hearts need to be softened. Dirt that is packed down and rocky is not a place to sow seeds of substance. As we walk together toward shared liberation, we can feel hardened, cynical, or "rocky." Foundations of faith and hope are essential to life and growth.

- *Patience*—Even with the perfect setting for a seed to take root, waiting is unavoidable. Under the surface, work is slow and unseen. It's easy to get frustrated and impatient. Commitment to the process and patience sustain the life above. You must learn to wait.

- *Resilience*—Every year, I begin my seeds in an indoor greenhouse and wait until the threat of Colorado snow passes before planting. Several springs have brought a series of hailstorms, which destroyed the small plants. Four months of efforts, gone. I had to wait until the next year to begin again. I have been a part of community efforts that have succeeded and more that have "failed." But each time we've come to a place of loss, we begin again.

- *Rootedness*—We need to remain planted and dig deeper roots within ourselves and each other. Strong, mature roots keep us planted and committed to the process of transformation regardless of what comes our way.

- *Celebration*—Celebrate regardless of what the year has brought; we can remain committed to join Christ's call to work toward the restoration of our broken world. We will reap a harvest if we don't give up (Galatians 6:9).

I will at times buy plants to speed up the process, but at the end of the day, and throughout the entire year, you can see seeds growing in dirt in my windowsills as a spiritual practice of holding the disciplines of faith and hope.

ONE DAY IT WILL BE OURS

The death of Michael Brown set off a chain of activism that is still moving forward today. His death was yet another reminder that we were not where we hoped we'd be by now. Racialized policing and killing Black bodies were still very present. Justice was not as close as we had hoped. We understood that even before the next video would be released, it was not a matter of *if* we would see another story of an unarmed Black man being murdered by police but *when*. George Floyd was one of a long line of people who died for being Black.

In moments of pain and grief, artists do what they do best—paint, write, sculpt, perform—bringing the pain of the moment to a shared place. Before Brown's death, which put the Black Lives Matter movement on a greater stage, film director Ava Marie DuVernay was putting the finishing touches on *Selma,* a historical drama that tells the story of the voting rights marches along the Edmund Pettus Bridge.[13] The film, which released three months after the death of Michael Brown, commemorated the fiftieth anniversary of that historic march.

Common, a rapper, and singer John Legend worked together to compose the film's theme song "Glory." As they penned the powerful words to remember all that was overcome for the rights of the Black community through those marching in 1965, they could not have anticipated the racial reckoning that was about to emerge because of events in 2015 around the time of the film's release.

A deep shadow had been cast at the death of Trayvon Martin in 2012 and the acquittal of George Zimmerman in 2013. The names of Michael Brown, Eric Gardner, Tamir Rice, Breonna Taylor, Elijah McClain, Ahmaud Arbery, and George Floyd had not even been uttered when this film was written and filmed, and the song penned. Filled with anticipation of what was yet to be achieved for racial justice, "Glory" became a song of the struggle to tell history as well as to drive healing and perseverance for the grief of the present. Within the long arc of the fight for Black civil rights, Ava, Common, and John could not have perceived what was about to unfold, even as they looked back to all that had been accomplished in those fifty years, with yet so much more to do.

> One day when the glory comes
> It will be ours. . . .
> The movement is a rhythm to us. . . .
> Justice for all just ain't specific enough. . . .
> The war is not over, victory isn't won. . . .
> We'll fight on to the finish, . . . when it's all done
> We'll cry glory, oh glory.[14]

As we consider the long work ahead, we count our costs to ensure that we can stay. We commit to work together, to do whatever is necessary until justice comes, knowing that one day the glory will be ours. In a collective chorus of the ages, we journey, joining those who have gone before us to "right the wrongs in history. No one can win the war individually." We remain committed, people defined by resilience.

"GLORY"

youtube.com/watch?v=O4gnunRKaXA

6

LEVERAGE WHAT YOU HAVE

AFTER YEARS OF SITTING AT TABLES as a dominant culture minority, working across faith and racial lines on behalf of the movement toward a more proximate justice, I began to realize that the only reason I was sitting there was to leverage what I had.

And what I had was privilege, specifically white privilege. I understood how to access and connect with people in power. I understood the cultural systems and was fluent in the cultural language. Privileged people looked at me as one of them. I was not easily dismissed. I had been brought up in a system of privilege, and while I no longer identified myself in the same ways, I had never lost the privileged roots that were indigenous to me.

It was at justice-work tables that I began to consider the power and influence of indigenous voice to indigenous voice. African Americans do not easily dismiss the perspective, experiences, and expertise of other African Americans; the same is true of other Black, Indigenous, and People of Color (BIPOC) groups. There are things that simply come more easily and are not denied among shared cultures.

I acknowledged that people from my cultural roots might not follow me, but as they listened, and even disagreed, they could not easily dismiss me. There was influence in that and I needed to use it as a force for good, to sow more deeply into the collective movement of justice.

A few years ago, I led a group of seasoned leaders on a "Hill visit." We flew in to Washington, DC, supplied training on legislative advocacy tactics, set up meetings with congressional leaders on Capitol Hill, and helped support their message of truth to power.

This was not just any group; these were leaders of community development organizations from across the country. They were connected to serious problems in poor neighborhoods, and with their faith centered, they were doing what they could to change the well-being of their neighbors. These were the exact kind of leaders that senators and representatives should be listening to. They had the moral high ground often lacking in politics. And, they had direct experience with some of the country's most pressing issues.

What I learned was that less than 10 percent of the group had ever done anything like a Hill visit before. These were new behaviors and practices. It was an honor to be a part of their learning curve. It was also an honor to grow alongside someone who was White like me.

Jeff felt very comfortable in Washington, DC. His cousin was a member in the US Senate. He had attended an Ivy League school, and powerful, influential people were his community. Though it had been a while since he had needed to speak in his native tongue and he felt some distance from his past, being in the epicenter of power he walked with a high level of understanding, fluidity, and confidence. His peers who were people of color did not have any of his advantages.

That day as they walked side by side, sitting in each office sharing their stories, he began to realize the differing power dynamics that were afforded the group. What he did not "catch," his loving friends helped frame, furthering his growth in solidarity and understanding of their limited access and authority compared with his.

After that day, Jeff and I debriefed, because for all of that shared multicultural and solidarity space, the reality was we understood each other better than anyone else in our group understood us.

As we talked and got to know each other, we shared some background stories, perspectives, struggles, and hope. Where we sat, we were often the only White leaders at the table, and we shared this unspoken understanding. We were indigenous leaders to the privileged, specifically white privileged, and all our shared grief and pain as we wrestled in BIPOC spaces came down to this one question: Why are we here?

"We are here to leverage our privilege and that is all," I shared.

The reality is our BIPOC friends do not need us to help them understand injustice and oppression. They don't need to hear stories or be educated on why systems are stacked against the poor and people of color. They don't need leadership. They need our solidarity and our cultural fluidity with those who look like us. Sure, on a personal level I could help with tactics and skills. But the moral authority, the personal stories of all of the good that needed to be shared, was all them. I helped support them to navigate places of power and influence so they could use their God-given talents and personal wisdom and their perspectives could be heard.

In our conversation, I told Jeff that we weren't sitting at the table to distance ourselves from a problem our people created and perpetuated. We weren't there to beef up our egos and get a false sense of assurance that at least we aren't like those *other* White people. We were certainly not there to grab selfies giving evidence to our BIPOC fluidity. These tables had power and influence, but had less access to formal power, and that was our purpose for being there. We were to utilize and leverage whatever power and influence we had with the privileged to make sure our shared message was heard and responded to. That was the only reason we were sitting there. Anything else was simply taking up space.

LET'S WORK TOGETHER UNTIL WE ARE ALL FREE

Lilla Watson is an activist, an artist, and a professor. She is Aborigine and works for her people's liberation. Watson's contribution toward activism and teaching is one of ensuring that those who join the work understand their place in it. She and other contemporaries, like Mary Graham, challenge and empower those who follow them to look at Western thinking and behavior from an outsider's perspective.[1]

Watson's investment with women, children, and aboriginal issues sparked new levels of awareness, which inevitably attracted others to join. She clearly understood a need for a collection of diverse champions to work together, but she also understood her own agency and the agency of the Aborigine people. From different spaces people could and should come together in an ongoing, respectful way on behalf of change.

In 1985, Lilla Watson spoke before the United Nations Decade for Women Conference in Nairobi, Kenya, and shared a powerful sentiment that spoke to the way allies could join their efforts: "If you have come here to help me you are wasting your time . . . but if you have come because your liberation is bound up in mind, then let us work together."[2]

When White people join up with Black Lives Matter, when Dreamers invite citizens to help them obtain a legal path forward, we form an understanding that people of the resistance don't need rescuing. So often those of us who join up and come to the table are so close to our own cultures that we are unable to be objective, leaving us defensive and disillusioned. This shared work is good work, but we need to be balanced. Those at the table can help us see our blind spots and craft a stronger shared space. We must respect those whose efforts we have joined and do what we can to make our shared efforts successful. We also need to see that ours is a shared liberation. I am reminded of the familiar quote, "Until we are all free, we are none of us free"—our freedom and liberation are intertwined.

Emma Lazarus (1849-1887) was a Jewish poet, writer, and activist who lived in New York during the mid-to-late 1800s.[3] She became aware of and then heavily involved in supporting indigent Jewish immigrants who were coming to the United States to escape the massacre and ethnic cleansing of Jewish people in Russia, known as *pogroms*. Lazarus used her platform to tell the truths of the moment and wake her people up to the atrocities impacting the Jewish community overseas. At the time, the Jewish community in the United States felt little responsibility to support the suffering and liberation of Jewish refugees fleeing Russia.

In what is referred to as the "Epistle to the Hebrews" she writes about the connectivity of their shared suffering and need for shared liberation:

I do not hesitate to say that our national defect is that we are not "tribal" enough; we have not sufficient solidarity to perceive that when the life and property of a Jew in the uttermost provinces of the Caucuses are attacked, the dignity of a Jew in free America is humiliated. We who are prosperous and independent have not sufficient homogeneity to champion on the ground of a common creed, common stock, a common history, a common heritage of misfortune, the rights of the lowest and poorest Jew-peddler who flees, for life and liberty of thought, from Slavonic mobs. *Until we are all free, we are none of us free.*[4]

While I do not want to promote a present day "tribalism" and I recognize the harm that it can do to humanity, Lazarus' sentiments were ones of resistance to awaken the conscious. She wanted her audience, her own people, to understand what activists such as Martin Luther King Jr., Fannie Lou Hamer, and Lilla Watson also came to preach—our freedom and liberation are bound up in each other: "Until we are all free, we are none of us free."

Shortly after she finished and published this epistle in 1883, she wrote another poem that year whose message would speak beyond certain racial and cultural leanings, of an aspirational place that would open their doors to everyone.

> "Keep, ancient lands, your storied pomp!" cries she
> With silent lips. "Give me your tired, your poor,
> Your huddled masses yearning to breathe free,
> The wretched refuse of your teeming shore.
> Send these, the homeless, tempest-tost to me,
> I lift my lamp beside the golden door!"[5]

This is an excerpt of her well-known poem, "The New Colossus," the poem that sits bronzed at the base of the Statue of Liberty.

DON'T JUST SIT THERE, BRING SOMETHING

Privilege is not something to simply recognize, but to share. This goes well beyond White or other racial privileges. People can benefit from privilege afforded because of gender, class, education level, socioeconomic status, religion, or ableism. Identifying our privilege and its intersectionality is important. When we consider the table, those with specific privileges can leverage those for the good of the whole.

Our purpose at the table is not to keep to ourselves the perspectives we are learning. This isn't some club that has formed to keep out those who don't agree. This effort has joined together to make change and we cannot simply sit there. Together we need to see the complements and strengths, and offer what is needed to support. If we don't know what we have to support, we can ask, inviting others to help us understand what is helpful and needed.

I grew up going to church potlucks. Church potlucks brought a cadre of dishes. To my childish eye and palate, some of the offerings were awesome and some were disgusting; if it was pink and fluffy, I was in; if it was green and stringy, I was out. I could bring my plate to the potluck table and pick and choose what would work for me. Everyone was invited to bring something. No contribution was rejected, but some dishes hit the spot with kids and not with adults, savory or sweet.

When I grew up and became a church leader, I became a seasoned potluck organizer. For some reason, gender aside, when it came to supporting the church potluck, I agreed to organize it. I happen to be a decent cook, but I am an unusual potluck organizer. I was happy to orchestrate when needed, but I had no interest in stressing over whether too many of one thing showed up and working to balance or boss others into what they should bring. I also expected everyone, even the young single guy right out of college, to bring something.

I really did not care if we ended up with twenty-five chocolate cakes and punch. I had a basic standard: bring what you can, and everyone bring something. It was not lost on me that in a group sprinkled with homeless people and overworked single moms, I might be stretching people. But I learned they liked to be stretched. I was always blown out of the water with what came to the table. Sure, we had our fair share of soda and hot Cheetos, but people were proud to bring what they had made. Some went to great lengths to bring things to offer.

I never tried to organize the contributions, but no one came empty-handed because everyone found something to give. The longer I lived and worshiped in communities impacted by poverty, the more convinced I became that everyone brings something, because I watched the dignity of people shine through in these humble ways. Repurposed food from the food pantry was going to show up, sometimes in the original can or box, but that was not the point—bringing something to the community potluck was.

I still use a particular saying when people who don't know me are invited to join another one of my potluck adventures: "My definition of a potluck is literal. Everyone bring a pot and hopefully we will get lucky!"

This is far from a perfect parallel, but I want you to understand that everyone brings something to the proverbial justice potluck. You are at the table to contribute something and not just sit there. Ask what is needed, offer what you have. Please keep balance in mind, however—there are no freeloaders and no one likes a show-off.

SPEAK UP

Sometimes God would use the voice of prophets to speak to those outside of the Jewish culture, but for the most part they spoke primarily to the Jewish people and leaders of the day. Because they had shared history, theology, cultural practices, and common memory with their audience, there was a high level of cultural fluency when they spoke. Those insider voices were hard to disregard and discredit, which was so upsetting to those who were listening.

Amos, a minor prophet tucked into the Old Testament, was a shepherd and a farmer of sycamore-fig trees in southern Judah before he began to prophesy. This shepherd-farmer was tapped on the shoulder by God to head to the northern kingdom and bring the word of the Lord. He left his quiet, country life and traveled to Bethel, a city where a temple was constructed as a place to both worship Yahweh and pagan gods. God called and said, "Go, prophesy to my people Israel" (Amos 7:15) and he did.

Amos served during the time of Jeroboam II, a successful king in the eyes of the world, regardless of how he achieved that success. The Israelites did not seem to mind that Jeroboam disregarded worshiping God alone or following God's law and justice for the poor. The people of Israel were trying to play both sides. They wanted to worship the gods of the day *and* Yahweh. They wanted to look out for their own interests and enjoy their wealth while denying justice to the poor.

Amos clearly understood and prophesied that to worship God meant absolute, singular worship. They could not worship any other God. To worship God was to love God and follow his commandments.

Amos minced no words as he declared to the privileged Israelites of the day, "You trample on the poor and force him to give you grain. . . . You oppress the righteous and take bribes and you deprive the poor of justice in the courts. Therefore *the prudent man keeps quiet in such times, for the times are evil*" (Amos 5:11-13 NIV 1984, emphasis added).

The times were defined by the status quo of injustice, and the smart thing to do was to allow it to happen and not speak up. Even when people knew they should speak up, it was not prudent or safe to do so! I see this and so many other parallels to present day. I wonder if people back then saw the problems and chose to keep quiet because they wanted to avoid conflict? I wonder if there was polarization between people who shared an origin, but they drifted far away from each other? Did they figure someone else would speak up? Did they think it was someone else's problem?

Regardless, they were content to allow the poor to be oppressed. They gathered in their house of worship, went through the worship practices that made them feel spiritual and righteous, yet went on disregarding justice. In that same chapter, Amos pushes against their small, performative practices of worship:

> I hate, I despise your religious festivals; your assemblies are a stench to me. Even though you bring me burnt offerings and grain offerings, I will not accept them. Though you bring choice fellowship offerings, I will have no regard for them. Away with the noise of your songs! I will not listen to the music of your harps. (Amos 5:21-23)

In essence, all those acts of worship when disconnected from the social and economic responsibilities of God's covenant became detestable to him and he didn't want any part of them! Powerful!

Amos goes on, "But let justice roll on like a river, righteousness like a never-failing stream" (Amos 5:24). This part of Amos is rich with calls for social justice and concern for the welfare of others. In the sacred and secular work of justice, this water metaphor of freely flowing justice may be one of the most familiar phrases, even if many do not know it is from the Bible! This metaphor creates a powerful image of waters generously flowing downward so that all can benefit from the assets.

The metaphor also pairs the words righteousness and justice together, a connection seen throughout Scripture. In Psalm 89:14 we see another metaphor utilizing this word pairing to describe God's throne: "Righteousness and justice are the foundation of your throne; love and faithfulness go before you." Here righteousness and justice are the foundation of God's throne, demonstrating the importance of God's values.

Righteousness, the Hebrew word *tsedaqah*, calls people to right actions beyond individual piety, encapsulating the rightness between people regardless of social differences. Justice, or *mishpat*, goes well beyond judgment for wrongdoing to include fairness and equity. Restoring people, structures, and systems to their most productive place, *mishpat* centers restoration of the whole, especially the poor. Where *tsedaqah* calls people to do what is right, those actions become *mishpat* when the people of God embody and put them into practice. To live a righteous life requires working toward the health and restoration of the whole, ensuring that people, regardless of wealth or station, have equitable societal structures.

Our liberation is connected. It's not okay if I and my family do well while others and entire communities and countries do not. Our wellness makes others well too. We are *supposed* to be connected to the well-being of others. Until we all are able to be free, we are not truly free.

HOARDERS BEWARE

It's easy to think that we don't have much to share. We may feel as though we are barely making it and no one is going to listen. We may have things to offer, but barriers of fear, anger, guilt, and shame keep us from jumping in. God gives us assets to steward, whether in opportunity, audience, platform, or financial resources, so let's leverage what we have with generosity. Those who are in relationship with us in the work, who do not have the same access or opportunities, can help us recognize and steward what we have. This is our core contribution at the table and one we should never resist!

We are all asked to share what we have been given and not to store it up for ourselves. Living a righteous life defined by doing justice does not include early retirement as an option!

Once, after Jesus taught about speaking boldly against the hypocrisy of the rulers of his day, he said, "Watch out! Be on your guard against all kinds of greed; life does not consist in an abundance of possessions." And then he told this parable:

> The ground of a certain rich man yielded an abundant harvest. . . . Then he said, "This is what I'll do. I will tear down my barns and build bigger ones, and there I will store my surplus grain. And I'll say to myself, 'You have plenty of grain laid up for many years. Take life easy; eat, drink and be merry.'" But God said to him, "You fool! This very night

your life will be demanded from you. Then who will get what you have prepared for yourself?" This is how it will be with whoever stores up things for themselves but is not rich toward God. (Luke 12:15-21)

In the work of faith-rooted activism it will be tempting to do some initial and generous investments, but to check out after a season. It's okay to a take a rest, a sabbatical, a vacation—you won't make it without taking time off—but those are temporary postures. God's invitation for us to join him in his work of restoration is ongoing, and we need to steward what we have been given until he says we are done.

IT'S NOT IN A LABEL

I was in DC with my friend and colleague Lisa Sharon Harper around the time her book *The Very Good Gospel* came out. I had not gotten a copy yet, so we walked to her office at Sojourners to get one.

It was 2016 and talk of racial justice was the banner. The phrase "White ally" had been thrown around a lot those days, so was "being woke" and "White fragility." These were words that were beginning to get new levels of traction, and frankly, they hadn't been well-defined for that moment. I am not entirely sure they are well-defined now either, because language is ever evolving.

As Lisa was signing her book for me, I mentioned something about being a "White ally." She stopped writing immediately, gave me a twisted look, and rebuked my comment: "You are no White ally, Michelle," and she went back to signing my book.

My mind began to spin: *Who was a White ally if not me?* I had been in the trenches of racial justice work alongside my neighbors for decades, boldly bringing my conviction of racial and economic justice to the public square. I was helping to lead a diverse, national organization on the top racial justice issues our country was facing. *What else would I need to do to become an ally?*

She finished signing a sweet, thoughtful note in my book, looked up, and finished her statement. "You aren't an ally; you are an *accomplice*. You aren't standing on the side, Michelle. You are in the jail cells with us."

Ooohhh, I thought to myself. I didn't even know that was a thing to be.

Labels can be helpful in identifying where we are and where we hope to be, but they can also be distracting and lead to a false sense of identity. Since that conversation with Lisa, our society and culture have identified new language to include the work of being a *co-conspirator* as another growing step of solidarity (*ally* → *accomplice* → *co-conspirator*). Who knows where the labels and branding will continue to move? They are not our focus. Let our actions and our willingness to keep moving toward whatever is necessary to reverse injustice define us, and let those in the movement help us better understand our identity.

THE NORTH STAR

Harriet Tubman was a revolutionary. After escaping from slavery, she became the most successful conductor of the Underground Railroad, affording freedom for countless slaves. It's no wonder she was dubbed a modern-day "Moses." A deep woman of faith, she believed that "God's time [was] always near. He set the North Star in the heavens; He gave me the strength in my limbs; He meant I should be free."[6]

It wasn't enough that she was free, but she also believed that she was to help liberate others too. "I was free; but there was no one to welcome me to the land of freedom. I was a stranger in a strange land; and my home after all, was down in Maryland; because my father, my mother, my brothers, and sisters, and friends were there. But I was free, and they should be free."[7]

Tubman and the Underground Railroad movement used songs and coded language to get messages to the slaves. Tubman often used songs like "Go Down Moses" and "Bound for the Promised Land" to signal that it was time to get ready to escape and so those escaping would know to get in the water to throw off traces of their movement. In singing these and other songs, she would slow down or quicken the tempo to help people know if it was safe to come out.[8]

Tubman's story has been told many times over. In 2019, Focus Features released the movie *Harriet*. The film documents how she stepped into her moment of history, found individual liberation, and then went on to liberate her people from slavery and oppression. The actress who played Harriet was Cynthia Erivo, an English singer and actress who worked hard to embody Harriet. She wanted to do more and joined Joshuah Campbell to write the closing song, "Stand Up."

> Stand up
> Take my people with me
> Together we are going
> To a brand new home
> Far across the river
> I hear freedom calling. . . .
> Gonna keep on keeping on. . . .
> I go to prepare a place for you[9]

Rania Aniftos of *Billboard* notes that the powerful lyrics chronicle themes of "hope, overcoming obstacles and kindness for others."[10] I believe it also speaks to faithful stewardship of shared liberation of one's people. We need to go to a new place together. Freedom, liberation, and love are calling, and we need to keep on keeping on. Jesus said, "I go and prepare a place for you" (John 14:3).

Bring what you have to the proverbial justice potluck. Share it boldly yet humbly. Do brave, public things, and make it clear that you stand on the side of justice. In the work of resistance never resist the request to leverage your privilege and influence your people. That is why you have been let in the door.

"STAND UP"

youtube.com/watch?v=TNO4omDaOEY

PROPHETS OF A FUTURE NOT OUR OWN, OR A PRAYER OF OSCAR ROMERO

A PRAYER BY FR. KEN UNTENER

It helps, now and then, to step back and take a long view.

The kingdom is not only beyond our efforts,

it is even beyond our vision.

We accomplish in our lifetime only a tiny fraction

of the magnificent enterprise that is God's work.

Nothing we do is complete,

which is a way of saying that the Kingdom always lies beyond us.

No statement says all that could be said.

No prayer fully expresses our faith.

No confession brings perfection.

No pastoral visit brings wholeness.

No program accomplishes the Church's mission.

No set of goals and objectives includes everything.

This is what we are about.

We plant the seeds that one day will grow.

We water seeds already planted,

knowing that they hold future promise.

We lay foundations that will need further development.

We provide yeast that produces effects far beyond our capabilities.

We cannot do everything,

and there is a sense of liberation in realizing that.

This enables us to do something,

and to do it very well.

It may be incomplete, but it is a beginning, a step along the way,

an opportunity for the Lord's grace to enter and do the rest.

We may never see the end results,

but that is the difference between the master builder and the worker.

We are workers, not master builders;

ministers, not messiahs.

We are prophets of a future not our own.

Amen.[1]

STEPS FORWARD TO STAY AT THE TABLE

1. Staying at the table is expensive. What costs have you had to consider? Are there costs you hadn't realized would be there? How have you oriented yourself to a long-haul work for justice?

2. Celebration is essential to staying engaged for the long work. Have you experienced any celebratory moments for justice?

3. Overcoming barriers that would discourage us and keep us from staying in the work is real. What are some barriers you have faced? How can you stay encouraged, bold, and engaged?

4. How have you had to be resilient? How have you seen people get back up after being pushed down? Are there experiences from others and/or yourself that have taught you resilience?

5. Intentional spiritual grounding is a must; prayer is mentioned as one key way to be resilient. Are there ways that you have seen or experienced prayer that keep you planted? What spiritual and personal disciplines help you be resilient?

6. How have you demonstrated unity? How have you seen it demonstrated? How do you want to demonstrate it in the future?

7. Can you see what you have that you can leverage? If not, ask those in the work what you have and if leveraging it would be helpful. What barriers exist to you leveraging what you have? How can you work to remove them so that you can boldly bring what you have?

8. How have you seen egos hinder the work? How are you ensuring that you are not caught up in showiness but instead are staying faithful to doing the work?

PART III

HELP YOUR PEOPLE

7

ROOTED IN LOVE

IN THE FIRST TWO PARTS OF THIS BOOK, I shared how to step into your faith-rooted activism journey, reorienting yourself to include and embrace new ideas, new spaces, new people, new ways of engagement. This third part also requires steps, but these steps begin by looking back from where we came as well as around to our present-day social circles. In looking back and around, we identify others who can come along and understand what we have come to understand—our faith compels us to join with others to actively work to restore and repair systems that perpetuate injustice.

As I shared in chapter six, we have not come this far to simply occupy space; we leverage what we have by using our voices in spaces where they may be received and where messages are not being given. We need people who come from our similar walks of life, communities, theological leanings, cultural understandings, and shared history to be engaged and join too.

In this third and final section, when I refer to helping "your people," think about what that means for you. Where are your roots? Who are your people? Who comes from similar starting points and needs to be influenced in ways you needed when you began to walk out? For me: my racial identity is one of whiteness; I have a Christian faith with both Catholic and evangelical roots; I originated from a socioeconomic class where everyone had advanced degrees, financial security, and identified with the Republican party; I am a woman, a wife, and a mother; I was educated as a teacher; I am a musician and worship leader; and the list can go on. There are multiple audiences I can influence in ongoing ways; you can too.

Take time to reflect on who your people are and how you might begin to bring them along in the work you are doing—not to become you, but to learn, be influenced, and join up in the good work of repairing and restoring broken systems.

As we consider who our people are, the idea of engaging them may evoke some powerful, unwanted emotions. It does for me. We may feel disappointment, fear, discouragement, betrayal, or grief. It's important to understand that the process of stepping out of the status quo is not a smooth, free, or easy transition. It can be riddled with pain, unintended consequences, and a high cost. And, while I don't want people to walk back into toxic relationships and compromise their mental and emotional health, there may be some important doors of bridge building that you can open to support the work of resistance.

In this day and age, we see high levels of polarization, especially around race and politics, and it can get personal fast. There is a huge divide along racial, political, and theological lines. In today's cancel culture, we are led to believe that people are too far gone for us to even attempt to build bridges. We can easily justify why not working to help our people engage in the fight against injustice is healthy.

I push back on that because I think we excuse ourselves too quickly. I believe building bridges back home is the work of those who follow Christ, who demonstrated love for us in emptying himself of his rights, privileges, and power to teach us a better way forward. This is the Christ we follow, and we join him in emptying ourselves of our rights, privileges, reputations, expectations, and even disappointments to walk a life that embodies love and forgiveness. To love the Father and to be about his kingdom here on earth means we don't withhold good when it is in our power to do good (Proverbs 3:27 and James 4:17). We don't get to burn bridges with no hope of redemption. We cannot hate enemies and we cannot be unforgiving to people, no matter how we are perceived in return (Matthew 5:43-45 and Luke 6:27-28).

If we believe in the power of restoration and redemption, we also must believe that no one is too far gone; anyone is able to join in the work of resistance. Everyone can reverse course and walk toward freedom and shared liberation. We must be willing to do what we can, where we can, to support the restoration process.

THE BEST OF ENEMIES

In 2019, the book *The Best of Enemies: Race and Redemption in the New South* by Osha Gray Davidson was released as the movie "Best of Enemies."[1] The film tells the story of an unlikely friendship between African American community organizer and civil rights activist Ann Atwater, and C. P. Ellis, president of the Klu Klux Klan in Durham, North Carolina. Forced to work together on desegregating their local public school, after some hard experiences these enemies began to see each other's humanity, their shared Christian faith, and the ways in which Ellis needed to repent of his white nationalism. Ellis had a complete turnaround and became a civil rights activist and union organizer! In an interview a few years before his death in 2005, Ellis shared, "When I joined the Klan, I thought every Black person in the country was evil and dirty. I just assumed it. We are taught these things as children, and when we get older, we sometimes carry those thoughts with us and never get rid of them."[2]

Loving enemies, working together to overcome hate, is a deeply spiritual work that *can* come to pass. At the end of Ellis' life he shared that he "considered his friendship with Atwater proof that anybody can change."[3] Their story is one of working to bridge racial divides against obvious divisions. We who are returning to help our own people scale a divide that is not as wide.

The work of justice is the long work of transformation, and helping our people is not exempt. It takes disciplined reflection to understand what we are inviting people into. It takes patience and forbearance to meet people where they are and bring them a little closer to a more just lens. It takes a commitment to love, forgive, and extend grace as we offer what we have learned. It takes healthy boundaries and a supportive community to discern when to try again and when to step away.

There is something else I want to communicate clearly: your "wokeness" is not an opportunity to perform or to belittle those who are not in the same place. This part of your work in the resistance is not to prove to BIPOC friends that you are better than other White people. It is not to separate yourself from your people so much that you put an adversarial distance between them and you. You are working toward reconciliation, not against it.

Be completely humble. Be adaptable, discerning but unrelenting, in your quest to lift the concerns of those impacted by injustice. Don't center yourself. Share and influence by pointing toward those in the work who have taught you. Share your journey with vulnerability, encouraging people to begin where they are and to lean in without shame. Biblical social justice that is rooted in honest action is motivated by love, and you cannot help a people you do not love.

FOR THE LOVE OF ONE

Jesus' life and ministry were at odds with the Pharisees. He drew big crowds, many of which the Pharisees considered the "wrong kind of people," like tax collectors and sinners. They had been leading in a way that kept people out, that intentionally sowed seeds of division and exclusion. Their leadership was the farthest thing from love and inclusion. In Luke 15 we hear the Pharisees muttering, "This man welcomes sinners and eats with them" (v. 2).

Jesus hears the Pharisees and begins to teach: "Suppose one of you has a hundred sheep and loses one of them. Doesn't he leave the ninety-nine in the open country and go after the lost sheep until he finds it?" (v. 4). And when he finds it, he calls his friends and neighbors to celebrate the good news!

Jesus continues, "Or suppose a woman has ten silver coins and loses one. Doesn't she light a lamp, sweep the house and search carefully until she finds it?" (v. 8). Once she finds it, she too tells all of her friends and neighbors to celebrate!

A few years back my close friend Theresa lost a diamond stud earring. A first-time mother at sixteen, with four more kids over the next decade, she and her husband worked hard to walk out of a life of violence and drugs, holding on to each other and Jesus, who they met along the journey. Since they didn't have some of the traditional celebrations and the symbols to mark them, decades later her husband bought her a pair of diamond earrings. One day when she was gardening, it fell off. She didn't realize it at first, but when she did, she began searching immediately. She called me and other family and friends to both console and pray with her that she would find this very treasured possession from her husband.

Months went by, and she would dig through rocks and bushes in search of the earring. She never gave up searching or praying. Then one day, she found it. Oh, the cries of joy! I remember her voice as she called to exclaim her good news. I shared with her the parable of the lost coin as we laughed and cried in celebration.

Jesus' parable resonates with those searching for, finding, and celebrating something they treasure: "In the same way, I tell you, there is rejoicing in the presence of the angels of God over one sinner who repents" (Luke 15:10).

Jesus paints a picture that each and every person is a valuable part of the kingdom. People aren't sheep or coins, but there is an earnestness that the table is not complete unless everyone is present. It's not enough to have ninety-nine out of one hundred— Jesus is going for a full 100 percent because he loves everyone, and no one is too far gone from redemption.

These two parables are followed by the familiar story about the prodigal son and his father:

> There was a man who had two sons. The younger one said to his father, "Father, give me my share of the estate." So he divided his property between them. . . . The younger son got together all he had, set off for a distant country and there squandered his wealth in wild living. After he had spent everything, there was a severe famine in that whole country, and he began to be in need. . . . So he got up and went to his father. But while he was still a long way off, his father saw

him and was filled with compassion for him; he ran to his son, threw his arms around him and kissed him. (Luke 15:11-20)

The father was so glad to see his son return that he ordered his servants to bring him a robe, put a ring on his finger and sandals on his feet. He even killed the fatted calf to celebrate, exclaiming, "For this son of mine was dead and is alive again; he was lost and is found" (v. 24).

Years ago, I remember sitting with my husband at a small church in South Carolina. We were on vacation and, as a church staff member at the time, my desire to go to a Sunday morning service was pretty nonexistent, but it was Father's Day and he wanted to go.

My body was there but my heart was struggling as I scrutinized the all-White, casually-attired congregation. I get pretty turned off by "cool Jesus" and that was the vibe of the place. These folks were excited to be reunited after a week apart and were chatting it up before the service. In my critique, I mentioned about how I appreciated a little more formality, what my husband referred to as "high church."

The virtues of high verses low church aside, the comment I made began a pretty ridiculous conversation between my husband and me. Back home, we belonged to a very informal church, and I loved it! I loved how people came as they were: the homeless, the addicted, the single mom and her kiddos, the defeated dad whose children don't know him, the disabled—all the people Jesus ate with when he was on earth. Ripped clothes were not a fashion statement but rather a reality—I loved my church!

What was my problem? Besides having to go to church on vacation, it was simply that I didn't like White evangelicals—my people. I was completely turned off by the worship, and I assumed from outward appearances that they did not want to seek Jesus and bring good news to the poor.

So here I was, in about the dumbest, most hypocritical conversation, yet my spouse patiently shared his heart and why he resisted "high church":

> Jesus is not as far off as people want to make him. When I was growing up, the idea of being a pastor or doing anything up front in church terrified me. I watched how you had to wear certain things and say specific words and phrases. You had to be some kind of person that I didn't think I could ever be.
>
> What was up front in my church represented the distance I felt and I think other people feel when they show up to meet God. I hate that, Michelle. Jesus loves them.
>
> When I think of the father in the prodigal son [story], with all his wealth and dignity, searching desperately every day to see if his son returned and then throwing up his fancy clothes and running as fast as he can to his dirty, disrespectful, wayward son, I want to cry. The love of the father is so deep and strong and close. I only want people to see that father. I want them to know that is how he feels and that they don't need to clean anything up or be a certain way to experience that love. He draws close to us as we are.

The two of us sat there in a room full of strangers with our heads bowed, crying. Crying because of a love that is so hard to comprehend, a faith that has so much extra baggage, and a world in desperate need to receive the free acceptance from a heavenly Father. He's such good news to everyone, including the poor.

That story of our conversation, of the parable and the tears in the moment, feel as real today as it did back then. My heart aches for the distance we put between God and those he loves. We put that distance in our own relationship with him and we stack up a lot of anti-Christ barriers so that we keep people from seeing and experiencing him fully.

God's love and acceptance are sometimes hard to receive, but it's even harder to see him give so freely. There are those of us who have followed and obeyed and sacrificed our relationships, our sense of our own belonging and identity, and have been all in to love the poor and see Christ in the immigrant. We have poured ourselves out in sacrifice and service to Christ and his kingdom. Therefore, we may be tempted to keep such a free love from those in the family who have played and squandered their lives, only living for their own comfort, safety, and freedom.

I want to do that. I want to keep Jesus and his love and gifts for myself and those I deem worthy. Sure, I'd love others to join, but those who are in the family yet misinterpret what it means to be an heir of the Father's kingdom and squander the best of the inheritance on foolish things of this world? No way, they can just stay away and pretend to be in the family. As for me, I don't care if they ever come home.

THE OLDER BROTHER

Several years back I was working on an advocacy campaign alongside my colleagues. As usual, we needed to work to bring in White evangelicals. Having roots to that faith tradition and being the only White person on the team, it was my job to provide insight and help navigate best practices to outreach to them.

At one of our meetings, I made some comment about how challenging White people were in general and my friend smiled. This was not the first time, nor would it be the last encounter of this sort. She chided, "I don't think I know anyone who is more prejudiced against their own people than you."

Yup, that was about it. I had walked so far away, gained a deeper perspective, and grew grief—masked as resentment against people from my roots—that was distinct and strong. Strong enough to be seen and called out. I did not try to defend or disagree with her, I simply let her words sit and sink in.

I was no different from those who were resisting reconciliation and justice for my friends of color or the poor. Here I was trying to build diverse coalitions to help reverse injustice, but I was holding contempt and unwillingness in my heart for people who looked like me.

I had a serious contempt problem. I did not want to love the people of my roots. I did not want to love the ones who disagreed with me, labeled me a liberal, disregarded the poor; but what is worse, I did not want to love the people who looked like me and *wanted* to join the work of resistance. I did not trust them. I doubted their sincerity and effectiveness, and unknowingly I wanted to circumvent their place in the movement by resisting them. I did not want to build bridges back to them. I did not want them to join at all.

The reality was the movement wasn't all that thrilled to bring them in for a lot of the same reasons I was skeptical. But I am White, come from privilege, yet have been poured into by communities of color to work together toward solidarity and justice. Who was I to create a wall to keep others like me out?

The parable of the lost son does not stop with the reunion of the lost son and his father but goes on to include an interaction between the father and the older son. The older son who stayed close to the father's heart, carefully tending to what he asked.

Meanwhile, the older son was in the field. When he came near the house, he heard music and dancing. So he called one of the servants and asked him what was going on. "Your brother has come," he replied, "and your father has killed the fattened calf because he has him back safe and sound." (Luke 15:25-27)

When the older brother hears this, he loses it! He gets so angry he will not even go into the party to celebrate. The father goes in search of the older brother and the older brother shares, "Look! All these years I've been slaving for you and never disobeyed your orders. Yet you never gave me even a young goat so I could celebrate with my friends. But when this son of yours who has squandered your property with prostitutes comes home, you kill the fattened calf for him!"(Luke 15:29-30).

All that anger, hurt, and betrayal. Was he really upset over a goat and celebration or was it deeper than that? The father pleads with him, "My son . . . you are always with me, and everything I have is yours. But we had to celebrate and be glad, because this brother of yours was dead and is alive again; he was lost and is found" (Luke 15:31-32).

Like the older brother, it was hard for me to extend my love and forgiveness to those in the family of God who exchanged the call of Christ's kingdom to live for themselves. In my journey, I watched siblings go different directions and held contempt in my heart. I have wanted to push them out and give up on them, but that is not of the Father nor is it of his kingdom. I cannot serve God and hold contempt in my heart for those he loves.

The circle isn't big enough, the table isn't complete without people of privilege, White or otherwise. We need people who look like me and come from my faith tradition to join the movement of resistance—not take over but join. Furthermore, it's not mine to protect or grant access to. In my recovery-of-blindness-to-sight journey, I was invited and afforded the opportunity to join. Others who want to should also have the chance. We must be motivated by love to help our people. We cannot help a people we do not love.

JONAH

During the time that Amos was prophesying about the future captivity of Israel, there was another well-known prophet prophesying—Jonah. Both prophets were bringing the word of the Lord during the reign of Jeroboam II (2 Kings 14:23-25).

Jonah in the belly of the big fish is one of the most popular biblical stories, up there with Noah and David and Goliath. Jonah gets called to Nineveh to tell the Ninevites to repent and turn from their wickedness. Jonah does not want to, so he goes the other way, as far away as possible. Jonah gets on a boat, gets thrown overboard, and gets swallowed by a fish. After three days of prayer, repentance, and worship to God, the fish spits Jonah up on the shore (Jonah 1:1–2:10).

God calls Jonah a second time to go to Nineveh, and this time Jonah obeys. He goes to Nineveh, the largest city in the Assyrian empire, known for their wicked lawlessness. The land mass is so big that it would take three days to walk across to deliver the message (Jonah 3:1-3).

Jonah shared the message from God, but you can tell he is simply going through the motions. His message is pretty brief—"Forty more days and Nineveh will be overthrown" (Jonah 3:4). Here's the amazing thing: on *day one* the word was received, believed, and spread quickly. A nationwide fast was put into place and everyone from the king to the cattle were covered in sackcloth, fasting and repenting of their wickedness (Jonah 3:5-6).

It's quite a remarkable story of conversion and repentance for the Ninevites as they turn from their wickedness and toward God. The saddest part of Jonah's story is that it did not end with his personal redemption—at least as we know it. The city was redeemed, the people were saved, and they turned from their wickedness for a season. (You can learn more about the future destruction of Nineveh in the book of Nahum.) But Jonah held contempt in his heart for Nineveh, despite their return to God; Jonah who did not want God to extend love and mercy toward people Jonah despised.

Personally, I have never cared for the prophet Jonah. He seems like a whiner whose life is characterized by judgment and a lack of love. But I have to wonder if my distance comes from the reality that I might be tempted to be that same person: I am a recovering, rich-in-spirit Pharisee.

The potential destruction of Nineveh and the call for Jonah to help bring about restoration to his enemies was a pretty big ask. Amos and other prophets typically brought a message from God to their own people. Jonah was being asked to go to a people he struggled to love and forgive. It is not an exact parallel to building bridges to our people, but it serves as a warning in the work of building bridges to people we struggle to care about.

The parable of the prodigal son and his older brother may not be the same comparison of the story of Jonah and Nineveh either, but we can have the same spirit of contempt in our hearts toward those who do not think or see the way we do. We cannot help a people we don't love. We need to love like the Father, who sees human value and potential and is searching for the opportunity to have people reconciled to him and to each other.

"Everything I have is yours," were the words the father spoke to the older brother. "Should I not be concerned about that great city?" were the words God spoke to Jonah. May we join the heart of the Father and extend love and grace to our fellow humans.

INVITE YOUR PEOPLE

I was at a recent gathering of national justice leaders who share Catholic and Protestant faith traditions. We were connecting around worship practices that sustain us, strategies and hopes for future policies and politics, and grief that the body of Christ was so divided on issues of race. The group was quite diverse. At one point, a sociologist shared how important it was to "get out of bubbles" and influence people who did not agree with us. For a few of us, that meant people from our past. We had social capital for connection, and common language and memory to make in-roads. We also had history of the work.

At that moment, one of the leaders in the movement mentioned his tiredness of trying to build bridges back home. I heard and connected to his pain. Just when a few people had almost given him a way out, Rev. Traci Blackmon spoke up. "Don't give up on that older generation, because they love you and they are hearing and being impacted in ways you don't understand."

Not everyone is going to follow our journey into a life defined by "all in" action, and that is okay. Not everyone we are bringing in comes from "the older generation." We may inspire some, but we are going to be in a better place to change the status quo if we inspire people to see the work, support it, and not actively oppose it.

We also need people cheering and supporting from the sidelines. In the work of engaging our people, we are inviting them to join and grow. This is probably a really big step and not one that we should quickly dismiss. We also never know how their stretching speaks to their spheres of influence, many of whom we cannot reach.

Early into my public-action life, I was part of leading and orchestrating an action at the Colorado State Capitol building as well as in several cities around the country. The event's message was the first of its kind: Evangelicals publicly stand with all immigrants in the United States regardless of immigration status. Pro-life meant pro-immigrant. Period. This event was not about abortion, but its message was to push back on the cultural stereotype that American evangelicals only care about the unborn.

A few hundred people gathered for this new expression of public witness. Christian church and nonprofit leaders who served the immigrant community were out in full force. It was an important line in the sand for what would grow to become a more national, grassroots evangelical presence in the immigration debate the following decade or so.

I invited my mom, Chris, who attended a large White megachurch in Douglas County, the third wealthiest county in the entire country, to attend the rally.[4] A nurse by profession, she had been volunteering once a week for years at the Inner City Health Center (ICHC) located in downtown Denver. For years she faithfully showed up every week at ICHC to serve alongside the staff there. She sincerely wanted to support the predominantly immigrant community who were patients there. Her experience had been a generally positive one, but outside of a few relationships with the nurses and doctors she was not making substantive relational connections with anyone beyond her culture of origin.

At the rally I was busy helping the speakers, connecting the media to those who were able to share effectively, and like any good activist mother, trying to wrangle and keep track of my three kids and their friends. I could not do more than wave to my mother from afar and keep the event moving forward.

My mom has agency so she did not need me to hold her hand, and she took her place in the crowd, not as someone who was seasoned in this kind of public witness but as someone who was curious and cared. As she stood in the crowd, she recognized the ICHC group and walked to stand alongside them.

Extending an invitation to her for this event was unfamiliar and unnatural for me. It was my first time asking her. It was also her first and only time to have participated in a public witness action on behalf of a political issue. That day she stood alongside familiar faces where she volunteered, listening intently and joining in our collective cry to bring about compassionate immigration reform. There was nothing notable that defined her participation, but her presence and willingness to learn a little more deeply made significant shifts in how she was perceived in her volunteer capacity.

The next week she went to the ICHC like she had for years, but because she attended the rally, others began to include her in their conversations. Over the course of the following months and years, she became a safe person to the group, listening to the pain and struggle of staff whose families were separated by deportation and an unjust immigration system. Her capacity to care for them grew in big ways and she joined them in new and intimate solidarity.

That was the one and only time my mother joined me for a public action but as a result she was never the same and her personal relationships were impacted in a very significant way. She not only shared new space with people at the ICHC, but she began to share with others in her small group and Bible study what she was learning.

To this day my mother cannot talk through the finer points of immigration policy or show her pictures of congressional meetings or marches she participated in, but she is still *with* us. She was invited in, and her eyes opened a little more that day. She carried shared pain a little more deeply, and no one in her immediate circle of influence doubts that she cares about immigrants and thinks they should too.

We need a big table to help influence change at every level, from the policy crafting tables at the US Capitol, to the kitchen tables of people like my mom. Those on the sidelines cheering us on inspire others in power who are resistant to do what they need to do—work toward the flourishing of all people.

Inviting my mom to join was a choice I had to make that was not second nature. I had built up defined walls to my former life and I needed to grow and actively work to bring down the barriers.

REDEMPTION, DEFINED BY LOVE

Being defined by love in action and looking for opportunities to build bridges toward something unfamiliar was exactly what Maria Francesca Cabrini, a young Italian woman, had in mind when she presented herself for ministry to the Daughters of the Sacred Heart. She wanted to serve, but was denied and told she was not healthy enough. Amid rejection, she was so sure of her calling that she formed her own Catholic order.[5]

In 1880 she founded the Missionaries of the Sacred Heart of Jesus, an order whose mission would be to be bearers of the love of Christ in the world. Thinking that she would follow in the footsteps of Saint Francis Xavier, the great apostle to the Orient, she went to meet with Pope Leo XIII and share her plan. She was about 30 years old at the time. What courage to persevere to get an audience with the Pope! He responded to her desire to head to the Orient with nuns of her order with, "Not to the East but to the West."

With those words, Mother Cabrini set aside her plans and instead headed to New York to work with her people—Italian immigrants who needed help and support in the United States. What began as orphan care and religious education in one city, led to the establishment of sixty-seven institutions that focused on healthcare, education, and other social services needed in poor, immigrant communities throughout North America, South America, and Europe.

Mother Cabrini was globally known for her work demonstrating and teaching social justice both formally and in her actions. She believed that extending love toward all was the only way to serve Christ. "Today love must not be hidden. It must be active, vibrant and true."[6]

Mother Cabrini, so committed to where she was sent, chose to become a US citizen and was the first US citizen to be canonized, as Saint Francis Xavier Cabrini, patron saint of immigrants. Her defining characteristic was her love for God and his leading her toward loving and bringing about justice for immigrants.

Mother Cabrini worked in direct service to people and is not thought of as a formal activist who shaped political change. But her public, honest action was on full display as she walked into a dangerous and emerging time in US history when xenophobia against Italian immigrants was at an all-time high.[7] Additionally, her leadership and service would come full circle and act as an agent to heal a deep pain in our racist US history.

In 1891, one year before Mother Cabrini arrived in the United States, one of the largest recorded lynchings in our country's history had taken place. New Orleans, Louisiana, home to hundreds of thousands of Italian immigrants, made international news as a mob, dissatisfied with the outcome of a murder trial, lynched eleven Italian men, nine who had just been acquitted in the trial of the murder of David Hennessy, NOLA's police chief, and two men who were in no way connected to the case.[8]

Between 1884 and 1924, nearly three hundred thousand Italians had emigrated to the city of New Orleans. Anti-Italian sentiment was running high all throughout the country at the time. In New Orleans, the largest enclave in the South, Italians were considered "culturally backward and racially suspect. Because of their dark skin they were often treated with the same contempt as Black people."[9]

The 1891 lynching sparked and further fueled anti-Italian and Catholic sentiment, and it threated the relationship between the Italian and US governments. In an effort to restore and appease Italy, President Harrison put two things into motion. First, he gave $25,000 to each of the eleven families who had lost a man to the lynching (setting a precedent for reparations), and through Presidential Proclamation incorporated a one-time holiday to lift up the contributions of Italians in American life. While many notable Italians were on the short list, with the upcoming four hundredth anniversary of Christopher Columbus' landing on what is essentially the Bahamas today, Columbus was chosen. Later it was named as a national holiday under President Roosevelt.[10]

For fifty years, Indigenous peoples and their allies have worked to end the celebration of Columbus Day, which remembers another Italian who came to the United States four hundred years before Mother Cabrini. Christopher Columbus was well-known for not only landing on the shores of North America by accident but also needing to make a profit. He captured and enslaved over one thousand Native Americans and Caribbean people. His brutal treatment of Indigenous peoples, from sexual assault and enslavement to torture for those who worked for him, has rightly led to calls to no longer recognize Columbus Day.[11] In 1989, South Dakota was the first state to replace it with Indigenous People's Day and several states have followed suit.

This has resulted in collective outcries from the Italian American community, not so much to laud Columbus as a great person, but to commemorate the community that worked so hard to be treated with equality and to have a day to celebrate their contributions. As an Italian American who is aware of our country's racist treatment of people like my father and grandparents, I want to remember their struggle, but not at the cost of lifting a person like Columbus.

The state of Colorado recognized the need to remove the celebration of Columbus yet remember the contributions of Italians to the United States' fabric. They chose to use that date to commemorate another Italian who poured out her life on behalf of the poor and marginalized. On October 11, 2020, Colorado replaced Columbus Day by instituting Cabrini Day in honor of Mother Cabrini, a faithful, Italian leader whose actions were defined by her care and concern for the flourishing of all people.[12]

Colorado's Cabrini Day Holiday Commission leaders Alisa Di-Giacomo and Steve O'Dorisio wanted people to understand that

> more than just a single day, Cabrini Day is a movement. Rooted in the kindness and compassion of the Italian American community, it is now a celebration for all to gather, give, share, and belong. It is a means to give back to our communities and make a positive impact. It is gratitude for what we have. It honors the opportunities afforded us by previous generations, paving the way through hard work, love, and sacrifice. It encourages learning, exploration, and growth. Cabrini Day is a path forward. A way to foster understanding, respect our differences, honor our commonality, and rejoice in our humanity.[13]

There is always redemption in even the most tragic stories. Mother Cabrini left a legacy that to this day is helping to heal a very public and historically dishonoring divide in my home state. I am glad to know Mother Cabrini's love still heals in both practical and public ways.

STAYED ON FREEDOM

My dear friend Walter Carmen and I have led worship alongside each other for years. Every time he sang, he would have us join him in the song "Woke Up This Morning (With My Mind Stayed On Freedom)," a freedom song from the civil rights movement. It was and remains his banner message. With a smile as wide as his face, he begins the familiar tune. Each time it is sung, he deposits the hopeful message of celebration and determination to keep our minds focused.

Recently I asked him where he learned the song and why he sang it with us. He shared that he was a young Black man in

Wichita, Kansas, coming to age during the movement for civil rights. Martin Luther King Jr. never came to Wichita, but other young Black leaders were working hard to integrate his hometown defined by segregation. He said he would hear that song on television, the radio, and on the streets, and as a young musician he learned it.

The song's roots were originally from the hymn "Woke Up This Morning (With My Mind Stayed on Jesus)." Reverend Robert Wesby of Aurora, Illinois, altered the lyrics to adapt to his time in the Hinds County jail when he was arrested during the freedom rides.[14]

Walter learned the song, interchanging "freedom" and "Jesus." At the end of the day, isn't it really the same thing? When we set our minds on Jesus, his love, his redemption, and his forgiveness bring forth freedom.

Woke up this morning with my mind stayed on freedom
Well I woke up this morning with my mind stayed on freedom
Hallelu, hallelu, hallelu, hallelu, hallelujah[15]

And it is with this steadfast mind stayed on the freedom that Jesus brings that we continue to help our people by committing to love them like the Father does, always in search of opportunities for reconciliation and restoration, rooted in love.

"WOKE UP THIS MORNING"

youtube.com/watch?v=ZLGXzGar7wY

8

ROOTED IN PEACE

SARAH GRIMKÉ WAS BORN INTO A WEALTHY, slave-owning family in Charleston, South Carolina, three-quarters of a century before slavery and the Civil War ended. I first heard of Sarah and her younger sister Angelina when I read *The Invention of Wings*.[1] I love to read, but without the help of lists like Oprah Winfrey's book club, I keep reading the same genres. Sue Monk Kidd's historical fiction of the Grimké sisters was one of those Oprah suggestions that I blindly borrowed from the library and read while I sat at the oceanfront soaking up vitamin D, sand and waves at my feet.

The deeper I got into the book, the more I began to realize that the experiences around Sarah and Angelina, who I thought were fictional characters, were lining up with the beginning of the women's movement in the Northeast. It didn't take long to realize that this was not fiction and though the author embellished the facts, the accounting was about real women who had walked away from their family's culture and way of life, intentionally working to undo its legacy.

Sarah knew from an early age that she did not approve of slavery. It may have been one of those pre-birth, prophetic determinations like Jeremiah 1:5 that compelled Sarah to head north and join the work of the abolitionist movement. Angelina would join her later. Their presence not only supported the movement from a different place but grew to build a bridge back home to influence the leadership of the South to end slavery.

Sarah and Angelina worked in tandem, traveling and speaking to women and men about slavery, faith, and the abolitionist movement. Speaking to women was acceptable, but when they began to speak to mixed audiences they were met with resistance. Nevertheless, they persisted and continued to speak out. Even though they spoke in northern states, they never forgot their roots and the unique voices and authority they had to "their people" to be heard and push for the end of slavery.

They became unable to travel safely in the South, so they reached out through written pamphlets to people with whom they believed they might have influence. In 1836 Sarah wrote a letter to the clergy of the southern states[2] and Angelina wrote an appeal to the Christian women of the South.[3] They knew that their faith had impacted them greatly and wanted to influence how the clergy and Christian women in the South thought about slavery.

In both of their letters, they shared their love and prayers for their southern home. They felt connected to their people even though their practice of faith and their view of social issues were no longer the same. They laid out a theological and moral argument against slavery. Both wrote in a tone that was humble, compassionate, yet unrelenting.

When it came to the practice of slavery, there was no confusion which side the Grimké sisters stood on:

This, my brethren, is slavery—this is what sublimates the atrocity of that act, which virtually says, I will as far as I am able destroy the image of God, blot him from creation as a man, and convert him into a thing—"a chattel personal." Can any crime, tremendous as is the history of human wickedness, compare in turpitude with this?[4]

However, they knew that they had come from what Angelina refers to "as branches of the same vine."[5] They understood that even though their letters would receive resistance, it was imperative that they reach out to share what they had learned. They provided solid theological insights to bring together a shared moral imperative—people are not property and chattel slavery must end.

Some of you have loved me as a relative, and some have felt bound to me in Christian sympathy, and Gospel fellowship; and even when compelled by a strong sense of duty, to break those outward bonds of union . . . you were generous enough to give me credit, for sincerity as a Christian, though you believed I had been most strangely deceived. . . . I ask you now, for the sake of former confidence and former friendship, to read the following pages in the spirit of calm investigation and fervent prayer. It is because you have known me, that I write thus unto you.[6]

The content of those letters is powerful. Clergy of the South had been using the Bible to justify slavery. Families who benefited from the southern culture held cultural and social beliefs that the Grimké sisters knew and fully understood. They were not "northern agitators" who were bringing beliefs from the outside. Their carefully framed arguments as well as their well-known life of Christian service to the needy, beyond the issue of slavery, made their words impossible to resist.

The Grimké sisters, mingling their faith with politics, were met with such tremendous resistance that they were unable to again step foot in the South, but their courage laid a foundation of influence that built up the abolitionist and women's rights movements.

Two years after their letters were distributed, Frederick Douglass, a slave, escaped to freedom and over time began to pick up the mantle of abolition, a prominent voice leading the country toward the end of slavery.

CREATING BRAVE SPACES

Charles Schulz, the creator of the comic strip *Peanuts*, introduced his audience to Linus. Linus, the sage of the Peanuts gang, is the younger brother of Lucy, the bossy, opinionated, and often bullish character of the cartoon. He is probably most recognized for dragging his security blanket around and sucking his thumb.

We meet Linus in the early years, but as he is developed, Linus becomes well-known for his belief in "The Great Pumpkin," a mysterious entity that comes to pumpkin patches on Halloween night to give presents to kids who believe. This story was later developed into the movie *It's the Great Pumpkin, Charlie Brown*, which aired for the first time in 1966 and still delights audiences.[7]

In the movie, Linus writes a letter to The Great Pumpkin much like a child would write a letter to Santa Claus. Friends try to discourage Linus from "believing." During one exchange, Charlie Brown walks away from the resistant Linus, saying, "We are obviously separated by denominational differences." Later his sister Lucy tries to bully him into quitting, and Linus reflects, "There are three things I have learned to never discuss with people: religion, politics, and the Great Pumpkin."

This adage of not speaking about religion or politics did not start with Linus, but this come-to-be-accepted truth was more popularized. The Great Pumpkin aside, it would be rare to find someone who does not culturally know not to bring up religion or politics. Personally, it's hard to avoid for our family, as my husband is a pastor and I work in politics and public policy. I often joke that when we walk in the door our very presence has a tendency to make people nervous.

Joking aside, if we are going to begin to make inroads with "our people" we need to be willing to bravely walk into conversations about what we are learning, even if they are socially and culturally uncomfortable. How we are engaging and how we would like others to consider stretching themselves to understand and come alongside are necessary parts of the work. In our efforts we need to be wise and peaceful stewards, or what I say is present-day "shrewd and winsome" (Matthew 10:16). Political commentating can be dangerous, laced with angry, destructive tones. Be shrewd where and how you engage. I have also found that a winsome person is completely disarming in helpful and unexpected ways!

I recently had the opportunity to lead an ad hoc board committee for a Christian nonprofit that I sit on the board for. We wanted to diversify our board intentionally and structurally. We had been successful with staff recruitment and the staff retention was impressive, but our board was majority White and male. The desire for the board to name the need and take the time to learn and put structural things in place was commendable. It's also fairly unusual, so for many this was an unfamiliar path.

The committee was made up of several board members, one who had strong ideas about what equity, diversity, and inclusion (EDI) was, and he wanted to be on that committee to ensure his voice was heard. The committee was open to all the board members and everyone's voice was welcomed, so that was not an issue.

When we began, I talked about creating a safe space to share and be heard. I talked about the value, perspective, and contribution of everyone. As the meetings went on, we began to really get to know each other and some of the deeper points of tension around EDI, specifically for this member. What was the biggest surprise to me was not that he had some unique and personal perspectives, but this space was the first place he had ever spoken them out loud. He had read materials, developed ideas and opinions, but had never had a community in which to process them. We were his first experience. (My advice, put your thoughts out there to see where they align with others. Be humble. Be a student. Fall on your face if you have to but get your ideas out of your head.)

Our group's outcomes had good success and accomplished its purpose, setting up a recruitment and retention structure to support EDI in the board selection process. One of my biggest takeaways from our time together was how in talking about and testing our opinions we helped shape each other, *all* of us. We all were able to hear different perspectives, shared values, and even dissenting voices with new compassion and vulnerability.

At our final meeting, the board member who had never had the opportunity to speak his thoughts in this area with others was getting much more comfortable with his newfound language. At one point I remember him saying, "I am a really conservative Christian guy. . . . I can't believe I am saying this, but I *know* social justice matters! It really matters!" We all joined him as he laughed, and we shook our heads because saying this out loud was new growth in him brought about by the efforts of our shared experience.

Practicing new words and concepts leads to new levels of understanding and conviction. It's important to engage important topics, even hot button issues like religion, politics, and racism. Helping people bridge those kinds of divides is the work of helping your people.

There is no safe or easy road to bridge building, but you can work to become a safe person and create safe spaces for learning. I have not always been that person or created that space; I am always working and growing in this area. I have found the work of author, researcher, and professor Brené Brown incredibly insightful—learning how to be a brave leader, creating productive spaces, and building empathy.

In her book *Dare to Lead*, Brown speaks to the bravery needed for hard conversations. "A brave leader is not someone who is armed with all the answers . . . who can facilitate a flawless discussion on hard topics. A brave leader is someone who says I see you. I hear you. I don't have to have all the answers, but I am going to keep listening and asking questions."[8]

In our divided world where everyone is self-protecting, drawing up sides, cancelling out dissent, and boosting egos, creating sincere, safe space for hard conversations is missing in our communities. This vulnerable, humble posture of genuinely listening and asking questions, not simply waiting to speak or argue, is what Brown affirms: "Choosing authenticity and worthiness is an absolute act of resistance."[9]

In creating productive spaces, we need to both understand and help others realize that the way we perceive things is "soldered to who we are." We need to honor others' "perspectives as truth even when they're different from ours."[10] Without the honoring of truth, there is no hope of reconciliation. Humble, vulnerable people create safe places for learning. They share vulnerably and humbly from their perspectives and experiences, allowing for other points of view to shape theirs.

When people begin to share, we also need to work to create a culture of empathy in the relationship. Empathy is being able to connect to the emotions of someone else's experience. We do not have the same experience, and typically when building bridges we are coming from different experiences and perspectives. Holding an open posture to other people and their emotions is essential to do the empathy work needed for restoration.

In our polarizing culture we are watching people hate each other and justify it. These aggressive, mob-like behaviors don't build anything except bigger walls of division, and that is not the work of a Christian. If we have to be better than, right, or the "knowers" in our relationships, Brown goes on to share, "we cannot be empathetic. And, to be clear (and kind), if we need to be knowers, empathy isn't the only loss. Because curiosity is the key."[11]

RACE-BAITING NOT NEEDED

Racism is another important conversation we need to engage with conviction. With all of the wars around race-baiting, from social media–driven culture wars to local school boards fighting about critical race theory (CRT), we may be tempted to avoid this essential conversation.

In my first book, *The Power of Proximity*, I share about the importance of understanding our history, our racial identity, how racism is embedded in systems and structures, and how we cannot do the work of reversing injustice by walking around this stretching conversation.[12] Posting "Black Lives Matter" on our social media thread or wearing a T-shirt with its message printed on it is not enough. It does send a message, but it doesn't adequately help communicate what it means to us or what we hope it can mean to others.

Regarding speaking to White people, my friend Daniel Hill has done a lot of writing on racism from a White context in his books *White Awake* and *White Lies*. In his most recent book *White Lies*, he has done a terrific job laying out nine practices to expose racism and the systems that perpetuate racism in personal and communal ways.[13] In the midst of so much good in his book, I find "Practice 6: Tell the Truth" to be exactly what our people desperately need. We all need to be free from the captivity of racial blindness to even begin to move forward toward transformation. Racial healing and transformation start with exposing lies and telling truths. Truth in our hearts and minds, truths in our relationships, and truths in societal structures.

Much of what Daniel shares around this centers on John 8:31-32. Jesus is talking about the defining characteristic of being his disciple. "If you hold to my teaching, you are really my disciples. Then you will know the truth, and the truth will set you free."

Daniel goes on to share about an interaction he had at a Christian college, where an entire row of students wore "Make America Great Again" hats and T-shirts. During the Q and A time of his presentation, a White female student shared her disagreement with him. Shaking, she began to admit that white supremacy may have been an issue in American history, but if he "looked around" now he will see that it no longer exists.

After the event was over, Daniel apologized to the Black college administrator about what had taken place with that student. The administrator refuted his apology and began to share his perspective:

> We find that White students are able to wrestle with just about every area of the Christian life. But, when the topic shifts to race, the entire mood changes. . . . When I talk about White Supremacy as a Black man, I know the students struggle with the truth. But many of them find a way to dismiss it because I am Black. . . . But, when you say the truth as a White male, it creates a different level of disruption. . . . I am glad [that student] was honest about how disgusted she was by the truth. I don't think transformation can happen until this resistance to the truth comes out into the open.[14]

On a personal level I do find it completely frustrating that a group of people who want to be defined by following Jesus, who called himself "The Truth," struggle and squirm when faced with it. This is why we must help our people face the truth.

I have watched this scenario play out in so many ways over the years. It's why I seek counsel before I invite BIPOC leaders into White spaces to share their perspective. I have often found that it's simply too traumatic for my BIPOC colleagues to continue to try. This is why White people need to be willing to share their journey and help other White people when it comes to race and privilege.

GROWING TIRED

Recently, I got off the phone with one my dearest friends, a BIPOC pastor and denominational leader. What she shared was not new, which is why she sounded so tired and irritated about her recent interaction. After spending the day in denominational meetings as the only woman and one of two BIPOC leaders in a group of thirteen, she was ready for some rest. As she walked out of the meeting, which had some racial elements in the agenda, her colleague looked at her and said, "I don't see color."

It wasn't a big part of the conversation or even the day, as she quickly dismissed him with a word—"I don't want to get into this right now." This brief account of her interaction is important to highlight as we transition to helping people with race. The reality is, getting into "this" is a huge part of what helping our people is all about.

Leaders of color in the movement get weary, and many are simply too exhausted to bridge build across racial divides. In addition to being on the front lines of reversing injustice, they are human beings with personal lives, families, marriages, kids, professional stress, limited resources . . . the list goes on. To add to that, they do the work often as a perpetual token or target of majority culture's whims. It's such a mantle to steward. They deserve our deepest respect and support.

That being said, our job in helping people is to help them understand the racial identity journey and why seeing color is so very important. Primarily we need to discern when leaders of color should be leading this conversation in White spaces and when they need a break; our friends in the movement can and should help us discern. Secondarily, we need to keep our blindness-to-sight journey in check, because no one is ever completely there; blindness to sight is a journey that we never stop walking.

This "helping" comes with strong warnings: we do not walk around, but we make sure we walk into the center with the right heart. We do not speak for directly impacted people. We do not speak for everyone in our racial, social, or gender class. We speak for ourselves and ourselves alone. We did not arrive at our conclusions in a vacuum. We never stop learning and growing.

In sharing our experiences, we point people to the leaders who shaped us, from Jesus to those in the work. We add our voices and speak with authority and experience, but not to center ourselves—our posture is one of constant redirecting toward directly impacted leadership. In this posture of leading, we *never become the leader*.

Even if we are the best of communicators, our message may simply not be received. But that doesn't mean it should not be shared. When we really love someone and believe they need to hear truth, we willingly offer it however we can.

The truth of Christ's life and witness was not met kindly by the leaders of the day. The Pharisees were out to get him, diligently studying the Bible in search of eternal life while missing the message that testified to the presence of the One who could give it (John 5:39).

Jesus was rejected in his power, truth, and authority. How can you anticipate anything but resistance to how you are sharing the truth of God's justice? Keep sharing the message. Don't pay attention to the critics. The work of resistance is met with unending skepticism and criticism. Jesus and John the Baptist were constantly being doubted and pushed.

To the closed ears and skepticism of those listening in his day, Jesus had this to say:

To what, then, can I compare the people of this generation? What are they like? They are like children sitting in the marketplace and calling out to each other: "We played the pipe for you, and you did not dance; we sang a dirge, and you did not cry." For John the Baptist came neither eating bread nor drinking wine, and you say, "He has a demon." The Son of Man came eating and drinking, and you say, "Here is a glutton and a drunkard, a friend of tax collectors and sinners." But wisdom is proved right by all her children. (Luke 7:31-35)

We need to be committed to our personal and collective transformation. Jesus is the Way forward, and while on earth the very leaders who should have shared what he had to offer killed him. You can try music, but some are not going to dance. You can give the most sobering lamentation, but they aren't going to mourn. God will restore what the locusts have eaten. Keep your hearts pure, repent with sincerity, seek justice with all you have. Wisdom is proved right, not by a few fickle kids, but by all her children.

FORGIVENESS, THE WAY TOWARD SHALOM

It was a cold, rainy night in DC. I was there to meet up with colleagues and friends to come together around the issue of immigration. In some ways it was a very familiar trip, but it was on the heels of a very challenging season for the organization I was working for. My body was tired, my heart was broken, and my mind was disoriented. It was hard to compartmentalize all that was going on in my personal and professional life. Much of that trip was a blur, but a cab ride with a friend and mentor, who was also on the board of directors for the organization I worked for, is something that I remember quite clearly.

My friend loved me. She saw me. She heard the anger and pain in my heart as we drove through that cold and rainy night. She kept trying to build a bridge to me, to provide insight, comfort, and even a little defense of where she sat in the midst of our shared struggles.

I remember wanting to have none of it. In the middle of her sentence, I very firmly shared, "I don't care what you have to say right now." I reminded her of organizational positioning and structures. I told her she wasn't safe, and that I didn't want to talk to her. "I am going to sit here in the back of this car in silence," I said.

There was a long pause of silence and then she broke it with something like: "You are really angry. You need to work on forgiveness. You should read *The Book of Forgiving* by Desmond Tutu."

My response? I'd love to be able to say it was: "Hey thanks, I will get on that." Instead it was: "I told you I wasn't talking to you."

I shake my head in disbelief at my unfiltered response and even chuckle at its undignified, immature nature. However, I am glad for friends and family in the shared work who tell me what I need to hear even when I specifically tell them I am not listening.

Here's the thing: I did listen, I made a mental note, and a couple of months later I ordered the book and intentionally chose to walk the wisdom and path of the book. I read it slowly, intentionally, and I grew. I decided that if Tutu could forgive his oppressors and lead an entire nation to work together to forgive devastating injustice, I could at least humble myself enough to read his book and learn from him. And learn I did.

The message of that book not only impacted me but transformed me. I found a way forward, not only for that situation, but for a broad spectrum of unresolved pain, helping me embrace the broken humanity of myself and others.

Archbishop Desmond Tutu was an Anglican cleric who was the Archbishop of Cape Town in the late 1980s. During his tenure, the South African anti-apartheid activist and leader Nelson Mandela was released from prison, in 1990. After that, Tutu and Mandela began to work together toward multi-racial democracy and to bring an end to South African apartheid.

Four years later Nelson Mandela became president and selected Tutu as the chairman of the Truth and Reconciliation Commission (TRC). The TRC's objectives were carried out in three committees that investigated past human right's abuses, worked toward the restoration of victims' dignity and restoration, and considered those applying for amnesty from their politically motivated actions.[15]

Tutu's message of forgiveness centers around walking what he calls the four-fold path: telling the story, naming the hurt, granting forgiveness, and renewing or releasing the relationship. "The four-fold path is a conversation that begins with a personal choice to heal and be free, a choice to seek peace and create a new story."[16] People harm people. This harm violates our humanity, demanding intentional restoration. What happens to us is often outside our control and not our responsibility, but "we can be responsible for what puts us back together again."[17]

What I found particularly helpful from Tutu's message was the connectedness of our shared humanity between both the victim and the perpetrator. Even though our distance between the other is wide, "we can find empathy and compassion. In finding empathy and compassion, we are able to move in the direction of forgiving."[18] We cannot remain stagnant and stop working toward restoration. If we cannot hear others and validate their perspective, "the forgiveness process will stall and [we] will both remain trapped in an endless loop of telling the story and naming the hurt. Empathy is the gateway to forgiveness for [us] and for the one [we] have harmed."[19]

The biblical word *peace*, or *shalom*, is much bigger than what we often associate peace to be: free from noise or even war. Shalom was the state that the world was created to be: connected, good, and in harmony with all things. Shalom is what present day activist and author Lisa Sharon Harper describes as "what the Kingdom of God looks like in context."[20] It's also what Martin Luther King Jr. cast as a vision for in his beloved community. Peace is not "the absence of tension; it is the presence of justice."[21]

In our striving toward the beloved community, the kingdom of God in context, we need to stop violating each other's dignity and instead work toward forgiveness, healing, and transformation. "Forgiveness opens the door to peace between people and opens the space for peace within each person. The victim cannot have peace without forgiving. The perpetuator will not have genuine peace while unforgiven."[22]

For Tutu, the message embodied the extreme importance of forgiveness and the steps that would not deny the truth of someone's pain all the way through to forgiveness toward the oppressor, even if that oppressor was not seeking restoration. Archbishop Desmond Tutu passed from this world to heaven the day after Christmas 2021. He left a lasting legacy of service, teaching us to be honest about the pain and brokenness caused between humanity, the truth-telling needed to seek restoration, and the unrelenting belief that shalom is possible. This well-respected, Christian faith leader moved his wounded people toward restoration and healing because of his leadership.

Forgiving the people in your story—including yourself—embracing our shared humanity and brokenness, and working toward healing and restoration open much-needed space for building shalom. Even if it is not reciprocated, for our own inner peace we need to open ourselves up to the possibility and practice of forgiveness.

THE PROMISE OF RESTORATION

The work of resistance can come with personal and relational sacrifice. Some relationships are never restored. Sometimes that sacrifice feels unredeemable. You may have the right humble posture, truly have empathy and compassion for your people, and deliver that truth with a sincere heart, and it still is not received. You need to leave that with God, the restorer of efforts and of "years the locusts have eaten" (Joel 2:25).

While scholars debate when the prophet Joel served the people of God, many believe it was at a time when the people had returned from exile and life was being lived without an appointed king. The years of Israel's rebellion, the exile, and the return are not lost on Joel. He reminds the elders of days gone by, when judgment came and destroyed what they had. He refers to locust swarms destroying everything in their path—a picture of a bleak time of destruction. Despite the destruction, Joel calls his audience to learn from their past mistakes, repent, and come back to the Lord.

He focuses on what repentance should look like: "Rend your heart and not your garments. Return to the LORD your God, for he is gracious and compassionate, slow to anger and abounding in love, and he relents from sending calamity" (Joel 2:13). Going through the motions of repentance is not going to set us on the right path. In this heart-rending, sincere repentance, God "may turn and relent and leave behind a blessing" (Joel 2:14). Joel talks about what the blessing could look like, what God's deliverance can provide. In our humble repentance, we don't have to be afraid but can instead be glad and rejoice. God will redeem what has been lost.

> I will repay you for the years the locusts have eaten. . . . You will have plenty to eat, until you are full, and you will praise the name of the LORD your God, who has worked wonders for you; never again will my people be shamed. (Joel 2:25-26)

God's restoration does not just include physical needs or an ability to praise God for his restoration, but he will go even farther to move his people to full reconciliation where brokenness is no longer present. God will deliver his people from injustice; he will be a refuge and a stronghold, and peace will be established.

This Spirit-directed restorative work we join defies human abilities, further demanding the work of the Spirit. His Spirit alive in us enables us to join his redemptive, restorative work. One day Joel and the other prophets would no longer be unique voices—one day the Spirit would fill men and women with prophetic, truth-telling words for restorative work in the world.

Peter references the prophet Joel's words in the second chapter of Acts, after the Holy Spirit descends on the people gathered for the celebration of Pentecost. "In the last days, God says, I will pour out my Spirit on all people. Your sons and daughters will prophesy, your young men will see visions, your old men will dream dreams. Even on my servants, both men and women, I will pour out my Spirit in those days, and they will prophesy" (Acts 2:17-18; see Joel 2:28-29). Filled with the truth of the Spirit, as active agents of salt and light in the world, we are to speak truth (prophesy), work toward justice, and become repairers of the breech, like Isaiah 58:12 says—all for the good work of bringing peace to our divided world.

A VISION OF HOPE

The year President Biden was inaugurated, 2021, our country was defined by division; broken because of political division rather than discord, sick and dying beyond the statistics of a one-hundred-year pandemic. However, on that day, a young twenty-two-year-old African American woman stepped to the podium wearing a bright yellow coat, which for so many symbolized a new ray of light, hope, and goodness.

Amanda Gorman, named the first National Youth Poet Laureate in 2017, shared her insight, her wit, her assessment of our shared struggle as a country, in melodic rhythm. As her words carried the tune of the spoken word, she inspired us with "The Hill We Climb." She spoke about choosing to put our future first by putting our differences aside, laying down weapons, and seeking harmony and peace for everyone. She called forward growth in our grief, to find hope in our hurt, so that together we will be victorious:

> If we're to live up to our own time, then victory won't lie in the blade,
> but in all the bridges we've made.
> That is the promise to glade, the hill we climb, if only we dare. . . .
> We will rebuild, reconcile, and recover. . . .
> For there is always light, if only we're brave enough to see it.
> If only we're brave enough to be it.[23]

And it is with this charge we lean more deeply into this young woman's prophetic and inspiring words to move forward. We choose to move forward in our quest to do the work of resistance, to persevere in our shared struggle toward shared liberation, to stay committed to our convictions of justice and to root down deeply toward the well of joy.

"THE HILL WE CLIMB"

youtube.com/watch?v=Xr9OvLZ8goM

9

ROOTED IN JOY

AS A STUDENT OF THE RESISTANCE in the movement of justice, defined by faithful service, seated at the table, and believing in the possibility of change, I can get tired.

I am not talking about deprived-from-sleep tired. I am not talking about take-a-vacation tired. I am talking about worn to the weariest, driest bone tired. Waves of deep sadness and grief can billow over me relentlessly and without mercy. Choosing hope, keeping the faith, knowing there is a cloud of faithful witnesses cheering me on are inspiring. Setting a vision of what can be and walking toward it believing that God is completing what he has started in a world *he* loves more than I do is the only way I know how to go. But I still get tired, so deeply tired. There have been times when I have reached serious points of despair.

Losing is painful. It makes us question our investments. It feels isolating, even in a sea of people who share the same heart and mind. If I were in the work for the immediate outcomes, successes, and feel-good victories, I would have given up long ago. I am in the work because the work is a good work. It's the honest, active, light-giving work of overcoming evil and pushing out darkness. This is what gives my journey and others' purpose, moving us forward despite what we see.

After a period of serious losses, personally and professionally, I realized I had lost my joy, that deep down exhale that I am held in the middle of a chaotic and broken world. My life was defined by many wonderful attributes of the Spirit, but joy was not one of them.

I shared this with a few close friends. I told them that people would be able to share with confidence that I exhibited love, peace, patience, kindness, gentleness, forbearance—so much forbearance and self-control. I did not believe, however, they would be able to testify that I had a life defined by joy.

My friends sat with me and didn't disagree but began to defend why I might not be very joyful: I worked every day in trenches of losing; circumstances in my community, across the country, and in the world were looking worse; hard things were happening professionally. It was the "Don't be too hard on yourself, Michelle" kind of encouragement.

It's nice to have friends who see you in your best light, but that is not what I was looking for. I leaned in more deeply, objecting. Joy is a fruit of the Spirit, I told them, it is not about circumstances. It is not about personal determination or discipline. Joy is something that the Holy Spirit gives when we are living a life in step with the Spirit. If other evidences of the Spirit were there and joy was missing, maybe I was quenching it or shutting it down.

The new year would be arriving in several months. I told my friends I was determined to pray that God would help me that next year to find my joy. I had lost my joy and I needed to find it. I couldn't alter my circumstances; I acknowledged my God-sized,

Spirit-filled request and began to pray, "God, will you help me find my joy?"

Through the months I shared with close friends about my quest. I told my kids and husband. I wasn't putting God to the test, but I also wasn't going to drum up joy to get my prayers answered. I needed something deeper.

I got a mentor that year who I knew would stretch my thinking and challenge me without reservation. I determined to use all my vacation time except what could be rolled over into the following year. I needed some personal lifestyle changes and was willing to do that work. I also needed new levels of pushback and challenge to how I approached my life. I had been living on the edge of frenetic for far too long. I eagerly invited trusted people to keep me accountable and to help me grow.

That year, while I worked to get my life into a more balanced place, I also was quite cognizant that it wasn't happening easily. Life in my immigrant community was the chronic target of hate and opposition. It was constantly eating away at the fabric of our shared hope.

TO CHOOSE HOPE

I was invited to join a group at the Mexican border for the twenty-fifth anniversary celebration of Las Posadas. Las Posadas, literally translated "The Inns," is a tradition four hundred years old held in Latin American cultures, taking place during the season of Advent.[1] In my majority Latino community, it is common to organize a Las Posadas celebration.

The event is a depiction of Mary and Joseph's journey to find room at the inn just before Jesus was born. Denied admission to every inn they pursued, the Las Posadas mass is a series of call and response readings and songs asking that the Christ child be given a place to be born.

In a neighborhood Las Posadas event, there is a processional in the streets, where participants knock on the doors of neighbors and the call and response message is shared. "Do you have room? Nope, keep moving forward. No room at the Inn." The processional moves onward until the group arrives to a place where they are welcomed in. The celebrations end with a party and piñata.

This time I was joining leaders from all across the country and Mexico for the twenty-fifth Las Posadas celebration at Friendship Park, San Diego. Friendship Park runs along the Tijuana-San Diego border. The border fences are divided by an area of land that Customs and Border Patrol officers will open a couple of times a year so that people can meet up and see each other across the Mexico-US border.

This cross-border Las Posadas event had been happening for twenty-five years when I stood with friends and colleagues on the US side in December 2018. Together we did the call and response back and forth at the border fence. It is always emotional to be at the border knowing the division, fear, and separation it represents to so many people in my community and communities all over the country. That day was especially emotional.

At the time, the US government was actively trying to deny entrance to those seeking asylum at our southern borders. The administration was only allowing a handful of immigrants to present their asylum cases each day. And by sending thousands of troops to the southern border or threatening to close the border entirely, the political climate was at a fevered pitch, further dividing our country into partisan sides.

Tent cities were being set up. Humanitarian efforts around the world were being directed to Mexico. On a personal level, I was so deeply grieved. It had been over a year trying to find my joy and I was still struggling. The darkness of the world was slowly snuffing out the possibility of the light of joy in my heart.

The day before the event, my college-aged son Alec and I joined my friend Sandy Ovalle over the border in Mexico. We went to a familiar place in Tijuana, La Casa del Migrante. It is a well-known shelter that houses people as they get ready to cross into the United States, or a place of refuge for those who have recently been deported. The space was packed to overflowing. Father Pat Murphey, the native New Yorker who directed the shelter, met us there.[2]

He told us, "We aren't playing Posadas here at the border. Anyone with a door has the ability to open it. Thousands of people are suffering and asking for help. You need to open the door."

I worked hard to keep my emotions at bay. He was right; my joyless heart was dying, I knew the anti-immigrant sentiment in the United States was worse than I had ever experienced, and the heart of the church was in no way better. It seemed that either complicity to the problem or harsh attitudes against immigrants were the only two options.

We left Father Pat's prophetic words and the mission he ran where the hands and feet of Christ were on full display, to go to another church housing a few families as they waited for an opportunity to cross the border and share their case for asylum.

At that church I met a family who had come from Honduras to the US border to flee political persecution and find safety. The father of the family shared the story of his travels. He and his wife left Honduras four months prior to travel with the safety of a migrant caravan. They drove until they could drive no more, and they had run out of money for food, eating in soup kitchens along the way. The father carried their two-year-old on his shoulders, their five-year-old daughter walked on her own, and the mother was five months pregnant.

They made it to Mexico City in two months, where the mother went into preterm labor and their third child was born. Each day the doctor and husband would go back and forth with this narrative: "When can we leave? We need to make it to the border."

"Your baby may not live until tomorrow. He needs to stay in the hospital."

"Can you guarantee he will live if he stays?"

"No."

Day after day this dialogue went back and forth until the family decided to leave the hospital and continue their journey, this time with the help of people in the United States who had learned of their circumstances.

At the time I met them, two months had passed. The father handed me his eight-week-old son and joyfully shared his journey. His enthusiasm was remarkable. The baby's due date had just about come. He was a healthy baby who looked nothing like a premature newborn. The father shared his story eagerly in Spanish. I listened and my son translated so we could catch each other's communication more fully.

"We are number 1,762," he proudly shared. Knowing they had waited months already and that the border was only processing a handful of applicants a day, I felt dizzy at the thought of his place in line.

He continued to share his hopes for a better life and how wonderful it will be when his family's number is called. I stood there with a plastered smile on my face as I intently listened. I prayed unspoken prayers over the life of his newborn son and their family. I felt like I was holding the baby Jesus, listening to a modern-day Mary and Joseph story.

How could this be happening? I thought. Father Pat's words rang so true—"We aren't playing Posadas here." As the man continued sharing his hopes and dreams, my heart and mind were racing. He was saying things like, "Tell Mr. Trump and the American people we are good people. Tell them we only want to work and keep our family safe."

Internally I was sinking to a very dark place. Thoughts of, "America hates you. They are never going to let you in" began to wage war in my mind as I prayed for their safety and my own soul. The sheer will to not scream out in pain, give back his son, and run as fast and as far away as I could took a strength in me I had never needed prior. I was a wreck.

As the room began to spin, I heard the voice of my friend and mentee Jenny Medrano in my head. Jenny is a Latina who lives in Denver and has shared some of her life and journey with me. "Never steal someone's *esperanza* [hope]," she would say. I felt so hopeless, yet this father stood before me so hopeful.

He had everything and nothing to lose at the same time by hoping. Hope, setting a vision of what could be, was the very deposit he needed to believe that his future would be brighter. I had everything I needed for a successful life. My children were born into privilege like me, and I pretty much got what I envisioned for my life. I was being asked in that moment to risk my disappointment of his losing by hoping with him. In listening, I was sharing his journey. By choosing to not steal his hope, knowing of his dark reality, I was joining him even if it was a struggle.

I will never forget that inward war with my mind and heart that day as I chose to join him in his hope. I left the encounter seeing his big faith in the impossible and my small faith. He had something deeper that I did not have. He was rich in hope and joy—two things I needed to find and cling to.

DEEPENING ROOTS

The next day was the gathering at the border. It was great to see friends from across the country as we walked the familiar mile along the beach to the border wall. All that had taken place in my heart and mind the day before had begun to take root. I realized that while I had grown and matured, I still had much more growing to do—my roots were too shallow. I needed to be like the tree that the psalmist refers to in chapter one, planted by streams of water.

With each step toward the border wall at Friendship Park, I began to see more clearly my need for deeper roots. Joy was there for the taking. The Holy Spirit's gift in the midst of the greatest life and death struggles was mine, if only I grew roots more deeply. My prayers began to shift as though my struggle to find joy had not been a couple of years in the making.

The service began in the familiar ways. There were songs and prayers going back and forth in Spanish and English across the border.

"En nombre del cielo, les pido posada, pues no puede andar mi esposa amada. . . . In the name of Heaven, I beg you for lodging, for she cannot walk my beloved wife." The Posadas song began with the traditional call from Joseph.

"Aquí no es mesón: sigan adelante. Yo no puedo abrir; no sea algún tunante. . . . This is not an inn so keep going; I cannot open; you may be bad people," responded the inn keeper.

On and on the songs were sung, moving toward the message of hope, of a child bringing a life of peace and justice to our broken space. Salvation to the world, a child was born, Christ the Lord.

I worshiped that day on the beach with new realization and new determination, to grow deeper roots in search of the waters of joy and allow it to defy my pain. I needed to open my eyes wide to the joy in the sunrise there to greet me every new, merciful morning. To open my ears to the cries of new life entering the world, proclaiming that new birth will not be stopped. To feel the soft petals of flowers unfolding. To drink it all in: dogs barking, children laughing, tomatoes ripening, grass growing, snow falling, life marching forward, despite the futile efforts of humanity working to darken its door.

Joy in all its fullness was there as it had always been. It was time to look up and out and around and to more fully allow the Spirit's water to flow down, deep beneath the soil to my roots, giving new levels of growth and stability. That rootedness would keep me planted in every season. The Spirit was there to help me get stronger and plant my roots more deeply so that the waters of joy could be soaked up, sustaining and enabling me to have a life characterized by joy.

As I reflected on roots, that underground work that stabilizes the tree above ground and affords it growth, I am reminded of our work of resistance. It's the under-the-ground, often unseen efforts that make a movement and its people strong and able to grow. There's the individual, personal work that each and every faith-rooted activist needs to do. We all need to make sure we have access to ongoing water; water is life and without it we stop growing and die. We need to ensure that the dirt is balanced and where there are blind spots and limitations, we need to seek out and add necessary elements to make sure the soil is rich and healthy. We need to ensure that sunlight is getting in by cutting back all that blocks those life-giving rays.

Interestingly enough, roots don't only grow when the tree is sprouting and displaying life, they also grow during the winter—that season when everything above ground looks like it is dead. Those of us watching, unable to see the roots, wonder if it will come back to life in the spring. It is during the cold, short-day and long-night season, when no evidence of life is seen, that the roots grow in search of water.

One day the work of resistance will come to an end. We know that the King is returning and that return is what keeps us going and brings us joy. We do not know the hour or the time but we do know that it will come. He will set all things right. He will establish a kingdom whose foundation is justice and all the work of bringing redemption to our broken world will cease. With this promise in our hearts, we are able to walk forward, rooted in joy.

THE KING IS RETURNING

In Matthew 25, Jesus lays out three parables that speak to how we should live in the liminal space of waiting between his first arrival and his return—the "day of the Lord" Joel spoke about.

First, Jesus explains the kingdom of heaven will be like "ten virgins who took their lamps and went out to meet the bridegroom. Five of them were foolish and five were wise" (vv. 1-2). The foolish ones took their lamps, but without oil. The wise ones had lamps and oil. The bridegroom called and, as you would suspect, the foolish brides' lamps had no oil for light; the foolish brides went to get oil. The bridegroom came, took the five wise brides who were ready, and shut the door. Jesus concludes,

"Therefore keep watch, because you do not know the day or the hour" (v. 13).

The bridegroom has been a long time in coming. We are waiting for his return, for him to right what is wrong and to establish his kingdom here on earth. We need to be ready to go at any time.

Then Jesus went on: the kingdom of God is also "like a man going on a journey, who called his servants and entrusted his wealth to them. To one he gave five bags of gold, to another two bags, and to another one bag, each according to his ability. Then he went on his journey" (vv. 14-15).

In this parable, two of the servants invested the gold while one buried it. The master returned after a long time away, and he saw that the two faithful servants who had invested had doubled the original amount. The master praised them both. But the master was not pleased with the servant who buried his gold: "You wicked, lazy servant! So you knew that I harvest where I have not sown and gather where I have not scattered seed? Well then, you should have put my money on deposit with the bankers, so that when I returned I would have received it back with interest" (vv. 26-27). At that the master took what the servant held and gave it to the one who had been given five bags of gold.

I have often heard this parable shared in the context of money. That God has given us all a variety of assets and if we don't invest them wisely, it's going to be bad news for the people who don't share what they have been given. I honestly do not know if Jesus was talking about worldly possessions or money, but I do agree that whatever we have been given from God needs to be received and reinvested in what God values.

When you look at the grave injustices of the world, and the ability to see the pain and oppression and join God in his work of redemption, I actually think that this parable is much broader than simply investing money. Maybe, just maybe, those who are poor in this world are the richest in what God has distributed and have more to invest in his kingdom while we wait for his return? Maybe those with the most talents to start with are actually poor? Maybe it's those in the back of the bus or the back of the line, or the last who become first, who can see the heart of God more easily? In Jesus' upside-down kingdom, where meek people inherit big stuff (the earth!), it would seem that the story might be a bit more upside down. I don't think the person who was given one talent to steward was financially poor in this life. Those who are rich in this life struggle to see the kingdom. It's not that they can't see it, but if it's easier for a camel to go through the eye of a needle than for a rich person to enter the kingdom, we need to consider more deeply how we invest.

Over and over again I bear witness to people who are closest to the pain of injustice continuing to hold joy. They see and experience deeply the pain of this world. They are rich in understanding and have little to lose in investing all they have been given. Those who are rich do not need God in the same way, one bag is more than enough. The rich have other things to depend on. Knowing God is a just God, and not understanding injustice in the same way as those who are impacted by it, they scramble to "fix" what is broken, fearing their efforts might not yield anything of substance.

My encouragement to the privileged is to stop scrambling and invest. Invest what you have been given and don't delay. In your limited perspective, throw off your fears and worries on how to invest your privilege as though it can be lost. It was never yours to have. Christ is coming, and with joy give back what has been given to you.

The final parable in Matthew 25 is a parable of sheep and goats. What we learn from the ten virgins is to be ready to go at any moment. The parable of the talents shows us that we need to not panic but invest what we have. The final of the three shows us *where* to invest: the hungry, the thirsty, the immigrant, the naked, the sick, and the prisoner. In loving and investing in the least of these, we intimately invest in Christ himself.

The parable begins: "When the Son of Man comes in his glory . . . all the nations will be gathered before him, and he will separate the people one from another as a shepherd separates the sheep from the goats. He will put the sheep on his right and the goats on his left" (vv. 31-33).

The sheep on his right, those blessed by God, are invited to receive their inheritance and enter his kingdom. The King shares that the sheep gave food to the hungry, water to the thirsty, welcomed the stranger, clothed the naked, cared for the sick, and remembered to visit the prisoner. The sheep ask the King when they saw him and did these many things. The King replies, "Truly I tell you, whatever you did for one of the least of these brothers and sisters of mine, you did for me" (v. 40).

After that the King says to the goats on his left, "Depart from me. . . . For I was hungry and you gave me nothing to eat, I was thirsty and you gave me nothing to drink, I was a stranger and you did not invite me in, I needed clothes and you did not clothe me, I was sick and in prison and you did not look after me" (vv. 41-43). The goats will ask, "Lord, when did we see you hungry or thirsty or a stranger or needing clothes or sick or in prison, and did not help you?" He will reply, "Truly I tell you, whatever you did not do for one of the least of these, you did not do for me" (vv. 44-45).

This is a hard parable—the punishment is eternal death. But the truth is, we need to invest in what God values. He is looking for those whose investment remembers and ministers to the poor, the hungry, the sick, the immigrant, and the prisoner. God wants us to see and extend mercy, care, and concern to anyone in need of mercy in this life, because we are doing it for him.

RUAH

The pandemic and global shutdown had been going on for a couple of months. The reality that familiar, in-person life was not going to return anytime soon had set in. At my job, I helped to support an annual national conference that typically takes two years of planning. Once the conference was shifted to an online format, it needed to rebrand and refocus. My colleague Lisa and I were tasked with discerning that new vision—and fast—as the conference was a few short months away.

The two of us talked, summarizing what was happening: a global pandemic that attacked the lungs, a national reckoning around racialized policing, a corrosive political environment with an upcoming national election. The year 2020 was the farthest thing from a clear vision.

"Lisa, is there anything that you think God is speaking to you about? Anything?" I asked.

"Honestly, I don't think I have much to offer. I do have one small thing. I keep thinking about the Hebrew word for breath—*Ruah*. It's the same word for the Holy Spirit. At a time when a disease is literally taking away our breath and George Floyd's cries of 'I can't breathe' are being repeated, I can't stop thinking of those two uses for the word *Ruah*."

That was all we needed to get moving forward. We were desperate for the breath of God to breathe in new ways. We were feeling so dead inside.

We went through the Bible story-by-story, recounting where the Spirit brought death to life: the stories of the Pentateuch, the kings of Israel, the books of poetry, and the prophets. Isaiah, Jeremiah, Ezekiel . . . we stopped and began to slowly read how the work of the Ruah set a vision of bringing death back to life.

Ezekiel understood what it was like to live with odds stacked against him and his people. Ezekiel is in the city of Jerusalem when the Babylonians attack. They take a first wave of exiles to Babylon, and Ezekiel is part of that first wave. A few years after Ezekiel is in exile, God calls to him and his prophetic life begins.

God speaks to Ezekiel in many visions and leads him to act out odd things to demonstrate the complete fall and destruction of Jerusalem and the temple. When Jerusalem falls, the temple destroyed, it is devastating for all of the Israelite people. It doesn't seem like there is a way forward. Maybe God will not preserve the line of David, maybe a king and a kingdom of peace are no longer going to be fulfilled?

We learn that after the fall of Jerusalem, God will make good on his promise to bring about peace. He uses the metaphor of a shepherd caring for and bringing his sheep to safety.

> I will make a covenant of peace with them and rid the land of savage beasts so that they may live in the wilderness and sleep in the forests in safety. . . . Then they will know that I, the LORD their God, am with them and that they . . . are my people. . . . You are my sheep, the sheep of my pasture, and I am your God, declares the Sovereign LORD. (Ezekiel 34:25, 30-31)

The reality of death and dying with a need for the Spirit of God to breath on people is as present now as when Ezekiel prophesied after the fall of Jerusalem. Everywhere people looked it was as though God had walked away from his people and his promise to them.

Then God shows Ezekiel a vision in a valley filled with dead, dry bones, in Ezekiel 37. This is not a vision depicting life recently ended, but bones that have been dead a long time. God begins to speak with Ezekiel.

"Son of man, can these bones live?" God asks.

Ezekiel responds, "Sovereign LORD, you alone know" (v. 3).

God tells Ezekiel to prophesy, or speak truth, to the bones.

Ezekiel does what he is told. "This is what the Sovereign LORD says to these bones: I will make breath enter you, and you will come to life. I will attach tendons to you and make flesh come upon you and cover you with skin; I will put breath in you, and you will come to life. Then you will know that I am the LORD" (vv. 5-7).

At that prophesy, Ezekiel hears a loud noise and the bones begin to crash together, tendons and muscles form, and skin covers them and they begin to look human, but no breath, no Ruah, is in them.

Then God said to Ezekiel, "Prophesy to the breath . . . and say to it, 'This is what the Sovereign LORD says: Come, breath, from the four winds and breathe into these slain, that they may live.' So I prophesied as he commanded me, and breath entered them; they came to life and stood up on their feet—a vast army" (vv. 9-10).

With the breath of God, man became a living soul at creation and at this vision of a dead army come to life. God was revealing to Ezekiel that the story was not over. In the midst of the driest of dry bones, because of his Spirit, his word still stands. We too are his sheep needing to hear those words, and just like the vision of Ezekiel and the dry bones, give our fears, our doubts, our exhaustion, our sadness and grief over to the God of redemption. We need to prophesy to the death and dying around us with the Spirit that gives us life.

> Prophesy—speak truth!—to the bones of pain
> and injustice that are ever present in the world.
> Prophesy—speak truth!—to the breath that can redeem,
> repair, and
> restore a unified army of the people of God for good work in
> the world.
> Prophesy—speak truth!—to the people so that they can
> give praise and lift up the
> name of the One who settles us in places of everlasting peace.

It was the Ruah of God that brought us to life at creation and it is Ruah that remains active, working in the world today to transform and set us on our feet. It is the work of Ruah that breathes life into a dead and dying people, reviving them army-strong, readying them to move forward together toward shared redemption and just repair.

WE WILL RIDE!

One of those army-strong, life-giving joyful people in my life was the indefatigable Carolyn Finnel. Carolyn was born with cerebral palsy. She was unable to walk or talk with ease. She had a sharp mind and a heart for God's justice. I met Carolyn in the mid-1990s at our church, Open Door Fellowship in Denver. She used a motorized wheelchair to get around, and we would see her all over downtown Denver in rain or shine getting to where she needed to be.

She led a support group for disabled people and their allies that was called "TRYAD," which stood for "To Reconcile You Able-bodied and Disabled." Carolyn loved to laugh and play jokes on people. She was clever and unsuspecting. She also had a huge heart for building bridges to people in the disabled community.

Her speech was a challenge to understand. It seemed I never got better at understanding what she was saying. She was so patient as she repeated her words over and over to my hard to hear ears. I remember when I first read something she had written; the words held so much. Flawless arguments linked together, written word by written word. Carolyn may have had trouble speaking, but there was nothing wrong with her communication skills.

Her writings and poetry helped communicate her heart and her powerful leadership. The humility with which she led was beyond inspiring, as she was so limited yet so resolved to stand up for the vulnerable, ensuring they were treated with dignity. She was stubborn and resilient.

Access to public transportation was not on the agendas of policy makers or the bus company in 1978. So she, along with eighteen other disabled friends from the Atlantis community, put themselves, wheelchairs and all, in a bus lane at Broadway and Colfax in downtown Denver.

That intersection, right by Colorado's State Capitol building, is a major artery to the downtown business area, and is one of the busiest intersections in the heart of the city. Together they protested, holding signs that read "Taxation Without Transportation." They blocked traffic and chanted, "We Will Ride!"[3]

They were arrested, and police taking disabled people in wheelchairs to jail became national news. Their protest got the attention of those who could make changes, and Denver became one of the first cities in the country to add wheelchair lifts to their buses.[4] Today, all across the country, public transportation has access for those in wheelchairs. That was not the way it was at one time. Carolyn and her friends used what they could—their own bodies—to transform a system and resist the status quo.

Their actions were the first of their kind and sparked similar actions across the country, resulting in the passage of the federal American with Disabilities Act, which transformed opportunities for the disabled community beyond public transportation.[5]

Our community said goodbye to Carolyn in 2006. I remember her funeral with my four-year-old son by my side, both of us looking at her casket. At that moment I was so proud to tell him of our friend's bravery, her brains, and her infectious laugh. It's good to learn from and lean on the strength of others.

That day back in 1978 Carolyn didn't know she and her eighteen friends were going to spark a national movement. She did know that the current stream that she was in did not work for the disabled community and they needed to make change. They deserved fair treatment and representation, and she wasn't going to let the status quo rule the day! Her willingness to get in the way, to make good trouble, and to resist her present reality paved a path for justice that others now take for granted.

SINGING JOY

That day at the Las Posadas gathering I had to leave early to catch a flight, so I was unable to be there for the entire program. Along with my son, I headed back down the beach, this time to walk without our group. As I turned I felt a new sense of freedom as the smallest sparks of joy began entering my heart. I felt a smile cross my face as I saw the Customs and Border Patrol agents standing with stern faces directed at our group. Before I left the scene, I intentionally stopped and shook the hands of each and every one of them, thanking them for their service and wishing them a "Merry Christmas."

There was no confusion as to whose side I was on; I was on the side of the immigrant. The counterprotesters, with their "America First" signs, only made the divide greater. Each agent responded to my greeting in a culturally acceptable way, but also with a little shock and disbelief. I was not only finding my joy at the border, but there I was practicing loving my enemies in new, practical ways.

As we headed toward the beach, my son remarked, "That was something to watch." Alec had no idea of my inner turmoil the past year. I responded with something about loving enemies and then began to share where I was in my quest to find my joy.

"Alec," I told him, "I understand that moms can be embarrassing and you may not want to walk beside me or even acknowledge what I am about to do, but I finally found my joy after a really long time of looking for it. I need to walk down this beach singing 'Joy to the World' at the top of my lungs. It's okay if you want to distance yourself from me."

Alec may not have understood the depth of my pain nor the sacred moment of singing my joy back into existence, but without hesitation he said, "There is no way I am missing this. I will sing with you."

So together, side by side with my young adult son, we belted out the words to "Joy to the World." We sang for joy that the earth received her King, of heaven and all of creation repeating joyous sounds. Joyfully we sang of how the King rules with truth and grace and justice, where wondrous love is sung by men and angels. It was such a time of healing for me. Nothing could rob me of my joy in that moment.

WE SHALL NOT BE MOVED

There may be so much wrong still in need of being righted, but the good work of change, even if slow, is happening. We see the effects of investments made by generations of people. We need to take time to look back and see how far we've come; there are things that can be celebrated even as we work to make more change.

I have this really great T-shirt that was given to me on Freedom Road's Ruby Woo Pilgrimage several years ago.[6] The shirt reads, "We are our foremother's wildest dreams." Every time I put it on I think of my Italian grandmother who, after she graduated from eighth grade, went to work in a sweat shop. Her life was defined by educational, financial, racial, and gender barriers that I cannot even imagine today. I am sure the generations that follow me will look back with similar sentiments because of the good work of those committed to reversing injustice.

We can celebrate today with women, with African American women, and with Asian American women on the election of our first female vice president. I think how Lucretia Mott and Ida B. Wells would be cheering at all the strides that have been made for American women's rights, even though there is still much work to be done. Migrants seeking asylum still face unjust barriers at our borders and we continue to work to change that reality; however, thousands of Afghan and Ukrainian refugees have had spaces open up in our country without punitive structural barriers.

Injustices big and small continue to be resisted. Dividing walls to relationships, like the Berlin Wall built across cultural and relational divides, continue to come down. Injustice does not repair itself, and we are privileged and honored to join those who have gone before us to work toward a more proximate justice for everyone.

Psalm 1:3 is a powerful metaphor of a tree planted by streams of water, with roots that are deep and nourished. Those roots connect to a life in the Spirit, submitted to his story of redemption, in his time producing fruit and healthy leaves. This is the deeply rooted, sustaining tree we need to be, deeply planted for a life of resistance work.

Our work is to carry the water just a little farther up the hill. Despite the long, exhausting journey that can feel disillusioning at times, with no guaranteed results in our lifetime, there is so much joy to be had. Planted near the waters that sustain us, our roots can deepen and grow. When the winds or drought come we can go deeper, knowing that we will not uproot.

We shall not, we shall not be moved.

Just like a tree planted by the water. We shall not be moved.[7]

This simple song, whose roots are from a time of slavery, is not credited to a specific author. Its message has been resurrected over and over again, well-known to the resistance. It has stood the test of time as we continue to sing and march to it today.

The biblical message of strong roots, planted by waters of joy, remains the steadfast message in the collective work of resistance, where our trees will bring forth fruit in season, with strong, healthy leaves. Deeply planted, we can trust that whatever we sow will be carried on and prosper.

When we uncompromisingly sing the hopeful message of what can be in the midst of our shared struggle, we deposit nourishment for the winding, unforeseen road ahead. Boldly speaking truth against the evil forces of complicity with the status quo is not only the work of the prophets of old, but one we must reignite in the message of today.

Standing on the brave shoulders of people who have gone before us, like Carolyn and those highlighted throughout this book, help us all better understand the honest action that is still needed today. Justice does not rule our day. So many people still sit at the margins, and we must join in the work of resistance to bring about change.

Jesus, the Redeemer, the Reconciler of all things, demonstrated what love is, setting a course forward. His kingdom will someday evidence its justice and peace for all. While on earth he taught us through parables, sermons, miracles, and human interactions how to boldly stand on the side of the poor and marginalized and against the leaders who were complicit and perpetuating bondage.

Someday justice will roll down like a river. Until then we have what we need to resist. Together we must join to work toward the collective good. Those of us who benefit from the status quo must not only cross over and serve the movement, stay at the table, and help our people. We must, as instruments of peace, do so rooted in joy.

"WE SHALL NOT BE MOVED"

youtube.com/watch?v=Qfovf6eV6JE

PEACE PRAYER OF SAINT FRANCIS

Lord, make me an instrument of your peace.

Where there is hatred let me sow love;

Where there is injury, pardon;

Where there is doubt, faith;

Where there is despair, hope;

Where there is darkness, light;

Where there is sadness, joy.

O Divine Master, grant that I may not so much seek

To be consoled as to console;

To be understood as to understand;

To be loved as to love.

For it is in giving that we receive;

It is in pardoning that we are pardoned;

And it is in dying that we are born to eternal life.

Amen.[1]

STEPS FORWARD TO HELP YOUR PEOPLE

1. What are barriers to loving your people well? How can they be removed? Have you overcome any barriers? What do you hope will be your story of bridge building?

2. Can you relate to the father and the older brother in the parable of the lost son? What can you do about loving your people well? Have you invited your people into joining your efforts? If yes, how did it go? If no, why? What are ways to invite them?

3. Have you experienced brave or curious spaces? What came out of them? If not, how can you cultivate this space? What kind of work do you need to do individually or collectively to foster these bridge-building spaces?

4. Are honesty and truth hard to see in justice work, specifically in the church? How have you seen honesty happen in constructive ways? How essential is forgiveness to the work of helping your people? How has it healed? Has it harmed? How can we learn from our experiences?

5. Can you relate to losing joy, hope, or peace amid resistance work? How did that feel? Are there ways that you can grow to more deeply root your joy?

6. The King is returning. What are ways you can invest now before his return? How do you want to be remembered? How can you help your people invest in Jesus' heart?

7. Are there songs in your heart that move you toward joy? Lament? Victory? Grief? How has singing them forward been a source of encouragement?

AFTERWORD

Dominique DuBois Gilliard

JOIN THE RESISTANCE is a clarion call to reckon with the fierce urgency of now! We are in a watershed moment where many people within and outside the church are asking interrogating questions about how our faith affects the world amid the brokenness and division that abounds. Many people are frankly questioning, "What is so good about the gospel?" and the tone of this question only intensifies within contexts where oppression, injustice, and trauma seem to reign.

Moreover, churches in the United States are shrinking, a growing number of pastors are quitting due to pandemic burnout, and young people are leaving congregations in unprecedented numbers. While these discouraging realities have caught much of the church off guard, Dr. Martin Luther King Jr. prophetically predicted some of this back in the 1960s. In a sermon recorded in *A Knock at Midnight* (Clayborne Carson and Peter Holloran, editors), King declared, "If the church does not recapture its prophetic zeal, it will become an irrelevant social club without moral or spiritual authority." This, unfortunately, is what too many people have concluded. So what do we do? And how do we change this?

John 13:34-35 gives us a blueprint. Jesus said, "A new command I give you: Love one another. As I have loved you, so you must love one another. By this everyone will know that you are my disciples, if you love one another." Therefore, what we actually have before us is a prime opportunity to love, and through that love, the chance to demonstrate—to a world that desperately needs to know—that something else is possible. We get to declare through how we live and love that the way that things are is not the way that they were intended to be. This is good news! But this good news comes with a cost.

Nothing allows us to display the love that Jesus calls us to in the new commandment like the Holy Spirit inspired choice to take on the mindset of Christ (see Philippians 2). The mindset of Christ compels us to love in selfless ways that are rooted in solidarity (as Jesus did on our behalf, but our solidarity is not salvific; only Jesus has the power to save!) and leads to us loving others as we were first loved by Christ. This countercultural nature of love (which leads to us sharing in the sufferings of Christ; see Romans 8:17, Philippians 3:10, 1 Peter 4:13) demonstrates to the world that we are Jesus' disciples. This Christlike love is best exemplified when we choose to enter into suffering that does not directly affect us, when we choose to enter in when everything around us says that we can turn a blind eye or simply pass by on the other side of the road to avoid the realities of injustice or oppression that are wounding our neighbors. This nature of love, rooted in solidarity, is compelling, evangelistic, and transformative. It will allow us to recapture our prophetic zeal and social relevance.

Michelle's first book, *The Power of Proximity*, explained that it is impossible to truly love our neighbors without being proximate to, and thus in relationship, with them. It also illustrated that authentically loving our neighbors requires not only building pipeline proximity but also relationships of mutuality. We must realize that we have something to learn from our neighbors, and if we are going to ever truly love them, we must also be intentional about learning their stories, histories, and plights. Thus *The Power of Proximity* helped us cultivate compassionate eyes to see our neighbors' suffering and empathetic ears to hear their anguished cries.

Join the Resistance builds on this foundation and moves into fostering tender hearts that respond to the broken in our communities. This book breaks down what it means to mature in Christ and embody a holistic understanding of the gospel. It helps us go beyond compassion and even mercy, to what the Lord requires of us—justice!

More specifically, this book clarifies what faithful allyship entails. True allyship requires consistency, humility, perseverance, and a conscious dependence upon the Holy Spirit. Faithful allyship is never about showing up to impart preconceived solutions. It necessitates listening, learning, and serving in all the unglamorous ways that garner no headlines.

There is a community development proverb that says, "Those closest to the problem are also closest to the solution." If we truly believe this proverb, this wisdom will alter how we show up, how we practice solidarity and defend the inherent dignity of our neighbors who suffer under the weight of systems, structures, and legislation marred by sin. This book gives allies marching orders and explains what it looks like to heed Scripture's call to be ambassadors of reconciliation and repairers of the breach.

ACKNOWLEDGMENTS

DISCIPLINING MYSELF TO WRITE THIS BOOK was one big act of resistance. Stepping out of the pandemic, transitioning from a job I loved, and launching my youngest into adulthood are just a few of the obstacles I faced when writing this manuscript. No book efforts are brought into the world in a vacuum—least of all mine! It is with profound gratitude for the harvest of champions who have supported me that I offer these acknowledgments.

Al Hsu, thank you for another chance to craft a message of kingdom justice to the church. To Patsy and Doug, Karen and Larry, thank you for affording me a place to get my thoughts written down. To Patty Pell, who listened to the earliest vision concepts, thank you for your scholarly and collegial support but most of all for cheering me onward. To my neighbors, friends, and the Westside Church Internacional and Open Door Ministries communities, you are the best group of mentors, friends, and family I could ask for. To Silvia Jordan, thank you for creating the beautiful piece of art expressing the good work of resistance, rooted in kingdom justice.

To Barbara Williams-Skinner, Mary Nelson, Alexia Salvatierra, and Kit Danley, I will be forever grateful for the collective wisdom you have poured into the work of kingdom justice. Thank you for supporting my personal growth and leadership as we all step up in new ways for a better, more just world.

To my chorus of champions, who probably do not even realize the level their voices and influence have had in shaping this specific message at this time in history—thank you! I have been listening. Thank you to Lorenzo Watson for always challenging us to define the work between marching; to Mayra Macedo-Nolan for telling me to help my people; to Michelle Higgins for ensuring that I tell people not to start anything new but to join; and to Michael-Ray Matthews, Terrance Hawkins, Dominique Gilliard, Jonathan Brooks, Lisa Sharon Harper, and Leroy Barber, who shared their perspectives and insights at just the right moment, always eager to do whatever is necessary for the work of kingdom justice. Many thanks to Dan Henley for encouraging me that the work is a slow work but we'll get there; to NL for his patient friendship and willingness to go deeper; to Agustin Quiles, whose tireless passion for justice is never satisfied; to Nikki Toyama-Szeto, who cheered forward my ideas with honest feedback and a smile; to Leslie Copeland Tune for sending me the message at just the right time that "the Christ child is ever present"; to Latasha Morrison, who encouraged me to "go with the people who are willing to go"; to Tina Mata, whose honest friendship brought water to my dry soul; to Penny Salazar-Phillips, who is willing to say yes to the next adventure; to Joy Athanasiou for her positive outlook and resolve; and to Kyle Giddings for doing whatever is needed to get done to support a friend in pursuit of justice.

To my daughter, Sydney, and friend Lisa Rodriguez Watson, whose calls and walks kept me visioning, writing, and creating, I could not have done this without your regular encouragement. To Alec, Wil, and Gixon for being proud of the work, and to David, who listens and carries the weight of injustice with me, who remains steadfast to ensure that things do not remain as they are, thank you. I love you all.

NOTES

1. WALKING IN

[1]Allyson Hobbs, "The Lorraine Motel and Martin Luther King," *The New Yorker*, January 18, 2016, www.newyorker.com/news/news-desk/the-lorraine-motel -and-martin-luther-king.

[2]Michelle Ferrigno Warren, *The Power of Proximity: Moving Beyond Awareness to Action* (Downers Grove, IL: InterVarsity Press, 2017), chapter 2.

[3]Peter P. Hinks, ed., *Encyclopedia of Antislavery and Abolition*, vol. 2 (Westport, CT: Greenwood Publishing Group, 2007), 759-60.

[4]Debra Michals, ed., "Lucretia Mott," National Women's History Museum, accessed February 10, 2022, www.womenshistory.org/education-resources /biographies/lucretia-mott.

[5]"We Are One in Spirit," by Peter Scholtes, *Hymnal for Young Christians*, F. E. L. Publications, 1966.

[6]Obituary for Peter R. Scholtes, accessed February 10, 2022, https://pscholtes .com/obituary.htm.

2. BRAVE STEPS

[1]"Micah," Insight for Living Ministries, accessed February 11, 2022, www .insight.org/resources/bible/the-minor-prophets/micah.

[2]Jenny Cox, "The Journey from Shittim to Gilgal," *Cross Connect* (blog), October 6, 2016, http://cross-connect.net.au/the-journey-from-shittim-to -gilgal/.

[3]"Lift Every Voice and Sing," NAACP, accessed February 11, 2022, www.naacp .org/naacp-history-lift-evry-voice-and-sing/.

4 Faith Karimi and A. J. Willingham, "What Makes 'Lift Every Voice and Sing' So Iconic," CNN, September 10, 2020, www.cnn.com/interactive/2020/09/us /lift-every-voice-and-sing-trnd/.

5 Karimi and Willingham, "What Makes 'Lift Every Voice and Sing.'"

6 "Lift Every Voice and Sing," by James Weldon Johnson, 1900.

7 Maya Angelou, *I Know Why the Caged Bird Sings* (New York: Random House, 2002), 179.

8 William Ernest Henley, "Invictus," Poetry Foundation, accessed February 11, 2022, www.poetryfoundation.org/poems/51642/invictus.

9 Angelou, *I Know Why the Caged Bird Sings*, 179-82.

10 "Lift Every Voice."

3. FALLING FORWARD

1 Nicolaus Mills, "She Scared L. B. J.," *New York Times*, February 7, 1993, www .nytimes.com/1993/02/07/books/she-scared-lbj.html.

2 Charles Marsh, *God's Long Summer: Stories of Faith and Civil Rights* (Princeton, NJ: Princeton University Press, 1997), 10-48.

3 "O Holy Night" by John Sullivan Dwight, 1855.

4 "Advantages and Disadvantages of Friction," DewWool, August 6, 2020, https:// dewwool.com/advantages-and-disadvantages-of-friction/.

5 Olivia Sanchez, "Lights for Liberty Immigration Protests over Border Camps Planned at 700 Cities July 12," *USA Today*, July 12, 2019, www.usatoday.com /story/news/nation/2019/07/12/lights-liberty-immigration-protests -planned-nationwide-july-12/1709905001/.

6 Conor McCormick-Cavanagh, "Activists Still Digesting What Happened at— and After—the Aurora Protest," Westword, July 17, 2019, www.westword .com/news/activists-digesting-what-happened-during-after-immigration -protest-in-aurora-11412967.

7 Conor McCormick-Cavanagh, "Fearing Deportation, Jeannette Vizguerra Re-enters Sanctuary in Denver," Westword, March 15, 2019, www.westword.com /news/fearing-deportation-jeanette-vizguerra-re-enters-sanctuary-in -denver-11270156.

8 John Blake, "The Voting Rights Martyr Who Divided America," CNN, February 28, 2013, www.cnn.com/2013/02/28/politics/civil-rights-viola-liuzzo/index .html; Donna Britt, "A White Mother Went to Alabama to Fight for Civil Rights. The Klan Killed Her for It," *Washington Post*, December 15, 2017, www.wash ingtonpost.com/news/retropolis/wp/2017/12/15/a-white-mother-went-to -alabama-to-fight-for-civil-rights-the-klan-killed-her-for-it.

[9]"Viola Liuzzo Memorial Marker," Encyclopedia of Alabama, accessed February 16, 2022, http://encyclopediaofalabama.org/article/m-3880; Julie Hinds and Micah Walker, "Detroit Statue Finds a Barefoot, Undaunted Viola Liuzzo Walking Again for Civil Rights," *Detroit Free Press*, July 23, 2019, www.freep .com/story/news/local/michigan/2019/07/23/statue-civil-rights-icon-viola -liuzzo-dedicated-detroit-park/1806238001/.

[10]"Keep Your Hand on the Plow," 1917.

THE COVENANT PRAYER

[1]Methodist Church, *The Book of Offices: Being the Orders of Service Autho-rised for Use in the Methodist Church, Together with the Order for Morning Prayer* (London: Methodist Publishing House, 1936).

4. THE LONG ARC

[1]Martin Luther King Jr., "Remaining Awake Through a Great Revolution," speech, March 31, 1968, transcript, See Me Online, accessed February 17, 2022, https://seemeonline.com/history/mlk-jr-awake.htm; Martin Luther King Jr., "Remaining Awake Through a Great Revolution," speech, March 31, 1968, audio, 46:39, https://youtu.be/SLsXZXJAURk.

[2]Theodore Parker, "Of Justice and the Conscience," from *Ten Sermons of Religion* (New York: C. S. Francis and Company, 1853), www.fusw.org/uploads/1/3/0/4 /13041662/of-justice-and-the-conscience.pdf.

[3]Alexia Salvatierra and Peter Goodwin Heltzel, *Faith-Rooted Organizing: Mobilizing the Church in Service to the World* (Downers Grove, IL: InterVarsity Press, 2014), 39.

[4]Salvatierra and Heltzel, *Faith-Rooted Organizing*, 39-40.

[5]Salvatierra and Heltzel, *Faith-Rooted Organizing*, 39.

[6]Angela Davis, "Interview with Angela Davis," *Frontline*, PBS, Spring 1997, www .pbs.org/wgbh/pages/frontline/shows/race/interviews/davis.html.

[7]Samuel Momodu, "Prathia Hall Wynn," Blackpast, October 10, 2020, www .blackpast.org/african-american-history/prathia-hall-wynn-1940-2002/.

[8]Martin Luther King Jr., "I Have a Dream," speech, August 28, 1963, American Rhetoric Top 100 Speeches, accessed February 17, 2022, www.american rhetoric.com/speeches/mlkihaveadream.htm.

[9]Rev. Raphael G. Warnock, "Prathia Hall Inspires MLK's 'I Have a Dream,'" clip from *The Black Church: This is Our Story, This is Our Song*, directed by Stacey Holman, produced by Henry Louis Gates, Jr. and Dyllan McGee, aired February 18, 2021, on PBS, www.pbs.org/video/prathia-halls-inspires-mlks-i -have-a-dream/.

[10]Frances Robles, "'We Are Nicaragua': Students Revolt, But Now Face a More Daunting Task," *New York Times*, April 27, 2018, www.nytimes.com/2018/04 /27/world/americas/nicaragua-students-protest.html.

[11]John Lewis (@repjohnlewis), Twitter, June 27, 2018, 11:15 a.m., https:// twitter.com/repjohnlewis/status/1011991303599607808?lang=en.

[12]Noah Adams, "The Inspiring Force of 'We Shall Overcome,'" NPR, August 28, 2013, www.npr.org/2013/08/28/216482943/the-inspiring-force-of-we-shall -overcome.

[13]"We Shall Overcome: The Story Behind the Song," The Kennedy Center, ac- cessed February 17, 2022, www.kennedy-center.org/education/resources-for -educators/classroom-resources/media-and-interactives/media/music/story -behind-the-song/the-story-behind-the-song/we-shall-overcome/.

[14]"We Shall Overcome at the Highlander Folk School," Southeast Tennessee Tourism Association, August 31, 2020, www.southeasttennessee.com/high lander-folk-school/.

[15]"We Shall Overcome," by Pete Seeger, 1947, adapted from "I'll Overcome Someday" by Rev. Dr. Charles Tindley, 1900.

5. RESILIENCE

[1]Donna Barber, *Bread for the Resistance: Forty Devotions for Justice People* (Downers Grove, IL: InterVarsity Press, 2019), 135-36.

[2]Mike Coffman, "The Time for Immigration Reform is Now," *Denver Post*, July 18, 2013, www.denverpost.com/2013/07/18/mike-coffman-the-time-for -immigration-reform-is-now/.

[3]Brian Bennett and Joseph Tanfani, "Immigration Reform Creates Odd Po- litical Alliances," *Los Angeles Times*, August 10, 2013, www.latimes.com /nation/la-xpm-2013-aug-10-la-na-immigration-money-20130811-story .html.

[4]Jack Jenkins, "This Missouri Pastor is Working to 'Reclaim the Language of Faith,'" *Think Progress* (blog), November 3, 2017, https://archive.think progress.org/rev-traci-blackmon-c81f140e144f/.

[5]Sandra Jordan, "Rev. Traci Blackmon Ministers at the Front Lines in Fer- guson," *The St. Louis American*, September 3, 2014, www.stlamerican.com /news/local_news/rev-traci-blackmon-ministers-at-the-front-lines-in -ferguson/article_854f8814-33cf-11e4-9de6-001a4bcf887a.html.

[6]Reverend Traci Blackmon, personal interview, January 31, 2022.

[7]"The Singing of 'God Bless America' on September 11, 2001," History, Art and Archives, United States House of Representatives, accessed February 18,

2022, https://history.house.gov/Historical-Highlights/2000-/The-singing -of-%E2%80%9CGod-Bless-America%E2%80%9D-on-September-11,-2001/.

[8]"Dr. Barbara Williams-Skinner" (bio), HuffPost, accessed February 18, 2022, www.huffpost.com/author/dr-barbara-williamsskinner.

[9]Dr. Barbara Williams-Skinner, *I Prayed, Now What? My Journey from No Faith to Deep Faith* (Baltimore: Fortune Publishing Group LLC, 2018), 167.

[10]Skinner, *I Prayed*, 168.

[11]Skinner, *I Prayed*, 173.

[12]This section is adapted from Michelle Warren, "Planting Seeds of Hope," Christian Community Development Association website, May 29, 2018, https://ccda.org/planting-seeds-hope/.

[13]*Selma*, directed by Ava Duvernay (Hollywood, CA: Paramount Pictures, 2014).

[14]John Legend and Common, "Glory" by John Legend, Common, and Rhymefest, *Selma*, Columbia Records, 2014.

6. LEVERAGE WHAT YOU HAVE

[1]"Aunty Lilla Watson," The University of Queensland, Australia (website), accessed February 22, 2022, https://alumni.uq.edu.au/story/13950/aunty-lilla-watson; and "Dr. Mary Graham," The University of Queensland, Australia (website), accessed February 22, 2022, https://polsis.uq.edu.au/profile/2235/mary-graham.

[2]Joanne Watson, "Lilla Watson," *Queensland Review* 14, no. 1 (2007): 47, https://doi.org/10.1017/S132181660000595X.

[3]Paula Hyman and Deborah Dash Moore, eds., "Emma Lazarus," Jewish Virtual Library, accessed February 22, 2022, www.jewishvirtuallibrary.org/emma -lazarus.

[4]Emma Lazarus, "A Quote from Epistle to the Hebrews," Jewish Women's Archive, accessed February 22, 2022, https://jwa.org/media/quote-from-epistle -to-hebrews, emphasis added.

[5]Emma Lazarus, "The New Colossus," Poetry Foundation, accessed March 2, 2022, www.poetryfoundation.org/poems/46550/the-new-colossus.

[6]Kate Clifford Larson, "Harriet Tubman Myths and Facts," Harriet Tubman Biography (website), accessed Februarry 23, 2022, www.harriettubmanbio graphy.com/harriet-tubman-myths-and-facts.html.

[7]Sarah H. Bradford, *Scenes in the Life of Harriet Tubman* (Auburn, NY: W. J. Moses, 1869), 20, https://docsouth.unc.edu/neh/bradford/bradford.html.

[8]"Songs of the Underground Railroad," Harriet Tubman Historical Society, accessed February 23, 2022, www.harriet-tubman.org/songs-of-the-under ground-railroad/.

[9]Cynthia Erivo, "Stand Up," by Cynthia Erivo and Joshuah Campbell, *Harriet*, Universal Music, 2019.

[10]Rania Aniftos, "Cynthia Erivo Delivers the Empowering 'Stand Up' for 'Harriet' Film: Exclusive," *Billboard*, November 8, 2019, www.billboard.com/articles /news/movies/8543078/cynthia-erivo-stand-up-harriet-film.

PROPHETS OF A FUTURE NOT OUR OWN, OR A PRAYER OF OSCAR ROMERO

[1]Ken Untener, "Prophets of a Future Not Our Own," United States Conference of Catholic Bishops, accessed February 23, 2022, www.usccb.org/prayer-and -worship/prayers-and-devotions/prayers/prophets-of-a-future-not-our-own; also referred to as the "Prayer of Oscar Romero."

7. ROOTED IN LOVE

[1]Osha Gray Davidson, *The Best of Enemies: Race and Redemption in the New South* (New York: Scribner, 1996); *The Best of Enemies*, directed by Robin Bissell (Burbank, CA: STX Films, 2019).

[2]"C. P. Ellis," *The Washington Post*, accessed February 24, 2022, www.washington post.com/archive/local/2005/11/10/cp-ellis/5beb7180-38de-4bc7-a49a -40234a4dc0b4/.

[3]Myrna Oliver, "C. P. Ellis, 78; Once a Klu Klux Klan Leader, He Became a Civil Rights Activist," *Los Angeles Times*, November 9, 2005, www.latimes.com /archives/la-xpm-2005-nov-09-me-ellis9-story.html.

[4]Amber Fisher, "Here's How Much People Make in The Richest County in Colorado," *Patch*, January 8, 2020, https://patch.com/colorado/littleton /here-s-how-much-people-make-richest-county-colorado.

[5]Michael R. Heinlein, "St. Frances Xavier Cabrini: A Saint for Immigrants," Simply Catholic (website), accessed March 2, 2022, https://simplycatholic .com/st-frances-xavier-cabrini/.

[6]St. Frances Cabrini Shrine NYC, cabrinishrine.org, accessed March 2, 2022, https://cabrinishrinenyc.org/.

[7]Nik Richard and Nick Weldon, "Madre Francesca Cabrini," *New Orleans Historical*, accessed March 2, 2022, https://neworleanshistorical.org/items/show/1442.

[8]Louis Nevaer, "The Lynching That Gave Us Columbus Day," *Medium*, June 18, 2020, https://medium.com/@nevaer1/the-lynching-that-gave-us-columbus -day-eb5179b01aca#_ftn1.

[9]Erin Blakemore, "The Grisly Story of One of America's Largest Lynchings," History, September 1, 2018, www.history.com/news/the-grisly-story-of -americas-largest-lynching.

[10]"Columbus Day 2021," History, October 7, 2021, www.history.com/topics /exploration/columbus-day.

[11]"12 Atrocities Committed by Christopher Columbus," Museum Facts, accessed March 2, 2022, www.museumfacts.co.uk/christopher-columbus/.

[12]Leif Townsend, "The First Monday in October in Colorado is Frances Xavier Cabrini Day. Here's Why the State Chose Her to Replace Columbus Day," CPR News, October 3, 2020, www.cpr.org/2020/10/03/monday-is-colorados-1st -mother-cabrini-day-heres-why-the-state-chose-her-to-replace-columbus -day/.

[13]Alisa DiGiacomo, personal interview, February 2, 2022.

[14]Allison Hussey, "5 Songs That Took on Tyranny Around the World, and the Stories Behind Them," *Pitchfork*, April 3, 2019, https://pitchfork.com /thepitch/5-songs-that-took-on-tyranny-around-the-world-and-the-stories -behind-them/.

[15]"Woke Up This Morning," by Reverend Robert Wesby, 1961.

8. ROOTED IN PEACE

[1]Sue Monk Kidd, *The Invention of Wings* (New York: Penguin Books, 2015).

[2]Sarah Moore Grimké, *An Epistle to the Clergy of the Southern States* (New York: s.n., 1836), https://bkbbphilly.org/sarah-grimke-epistle-clergy-southern-states.

[3]Angelina Emily Grimké, *An Appeal to the Christian Women of the South* (New York: American Anti-Slavery Society, 1836), www.loc.gov/item/11007392/.

[4]Grimké, *An Epistle to the Clergy*.

[5]Grimké, *An Appeal to the Christian Women*.

[6]Grimké, *An Appeal to the Christian Women*.

[7]*It's the Great Pumpkin, Charlie Brown*, directed by Bill Melendez, aired October 27, 1966, on CBS.

[8]Brené Brown, *Dare to Lead: Brave Work, Tough Conversations, Whole Hearts* (New York: Random House, 2018), 194.

[9]Brown, *Dare to Lead*, 271.

[10]Brown, *Dare to Lead*, 143.

[11]Brown, *Dare to Lead*, 145.

[12]Michelle Ferrigno Warren, *The Power of Proximity: Moving Beyond Awareness to Action* (Downers Grove, IL: InterVarsity Press, 2017), chapter 5.

[13]Daniel Hill, *White Lies* (Grand Rapids, MI: Zondervan, 2020).

[14]Hill, *White Lies*, 147.

[15]Truth and Reconciliation Commission (website), accessed February 28, 2022, www.justice.gov.za/trc/trccom.html.

[16]Desmond Tutu and Mpho A. Tutu, *The Book of Forgiving: The Fourfold Path for Healing Ourselves and Our World* (New York: HarperOne, 2014), 54.

[17]Tutu, *The Book of Forgiving*, 97.

[18]Tutu, *The Book of Forgiving*, 127.

[19]Tutu, *The Book of Forgiving*, 179.

[20]Lisa Sharon Harper, *The Very Good Gospel: How Everything Wrong Can Be Made Right* (Colorado Springs, CO: WaterBrook, 2016), 13-14.

[21]"Quotations," Martin Luther King Jr. Memorial (website), accessed February 28, 2022, www.nps.gov/mlkm/learn/quotations.htm.

[22]Tutu, *The Book of Forgiving*, 25.

[23]Amanda Gorman, *The Hill We Climb: An Inaugural Poem for the Country* (New York: Viking, 2021).

9. ROOTED IN JOY

[1]Editors of Encyclopaedia, "Las Posadas," *Encyclopedia Britannica*, October 16, 2021, www.britannica.com/topic/Las-Posadas.

[2]Sandra Dibble, "US Priest Directs Tijuana Migrant Shelter," *The San Diego Union-Tribune*, August 7, 2013, www.sandiegouniontribune.com/news/border -baja-california/sdut-us-priest-tijuana-migrant-immigration-reform-2013 aug07-story.html.

[3]Kyle Cooke, "We Will Ride: 43 Years After the 'Gang of 19' Protests," Rocky Mountain PBS, July 5, 2021, www.rmpbs.org/blogs/rocky-mountain-pbs /gang-of-19-43-year-anniversary/.

[4]Cooke, "We Will Ride."

[5]Virginia Culver, "Disabled Activist Became a Force for Change," *The Denver Post*, July 5, 2006, www.denverpost.com/2006/07/05/disabled-activist-became -a-force-for-change/.

[6]"Freedom Road Pilgrimages," Freedom Road (website), accessed March 2, 2022, https://freedomroad.us/what-we-do/freedom-road-pilgrimages/.

[7]"We Shall Not Be Moved," adapted from "I Shall Not Be Moved," by Alfred H. Ackley, 1906.

PEACE PRAYER OF SAINT FRANCIS

[1]Saint Francis, "Peace Prayer of Saint Francis," Loyola Press, accessed March 2, 2022, www.loyolapress.com/catholic-resources/prayer/traditional-catholic -prayers/saints-prayers/peace-prayer-of-saint-francis/.

ALSO BY MICHELLE FERRIGNO WARREN

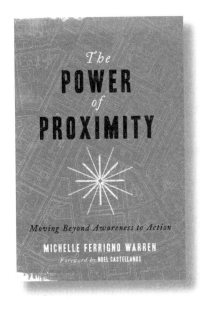

The Power of Proximity

978-0-8308-4390-9

C|C CHRISTIAN COMMUNITY
D|A DEVELOPMENT ASSOCIATION

The Christian Community Development Association (CCDA) is a network of Christians committed to engaging with people and communities in the process of transformation. For over twenty-five years, CCDA has aimed to inspire, train, and connect Christians who seek to bear witness to the Kingdom of God by reclaiming and restoring under-resourced communities. CCDA walks alongside local practitioners and partners as they live out Christian Community Development (CCD) by loving their neighbors.

CCDA was founded in 1989 under the leadership of Dr. John Perkins and several other key leaders who are engaged in the work of Christian Community Development still today. Since then, practitioners and partners engaged in the work of the Kingdom have taken ownership of the movement. Our diverse membership and the breadth of the CCDA family are integral to realizing the vision of restored communities.

The CCDA National Conference was birthed as an annual opportunity for practitioners and partners engaged in CCD to gather, sharing best practices and seeking encouragement, inspiration, and connection to other like-minded Christ-followers, committed to ministry in difficult places. For four days, the CCDA family, coming from across the country and around the world, is reunited around a common vision and heart.

Additionally, the CCDA Institute serves as the educational and training arm of the association, offering workshops and trainings in the philosophy of CCD. We have created a space for diverse groups of leaders to be steeped in the heart of CCD and forge lifelong friendships over the course of two years through CCDA's Leadership Cohort.

CCDA has a long-standing commitment to the confrontation of injustice. Our advocacy and organizing is rooted in Jesus' compassion and commitment to Kingdom justice. While we recognize there are many injustices to be fought, as an association we are strategically working on issues of immigration, mass incarceration, and education reform.

To learn more, visit www.ccda.org/ivp

TITLES FROM CCDA

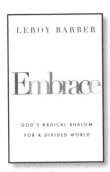

Embrace
978-0-8308-4471-5

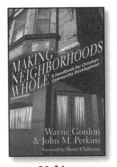

**Making
Neighborhoods Whole**
978-0-8308-3756-4

Brown Church
978-0-8308-5285-7

Uncommon Church
978-0-8308-4162-2

**Rethinking
Incarceration**
978-0-8308-4529-3

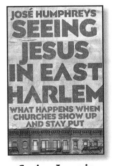

**Seeing Jesus in
East Harlem**
978-0-8308-4149-3

**Welcoming Justice
(expanded edition)**
978-0-8308-3479-2

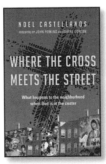

**Where the Cross
Meets the Street**
978-0-8308-3691-8

White Awake
978-0-8308-4393-0

Missio Alliance

and

ĩvp | InterVarsity Press

Missio Alliance has arisen in response to the shared voice of pastors and ministry leaders from across the landscape of North American Christianity for a new "space" of togetherness and reflection amid the issues and challenges facing the church in our day. We are united by a desire for a fresh expression of evangelical faith, one significantly informed by the global evangelical family. Lausanne's Cape Town Commitment, "A Confession of Faith and a Call to Action," provides an excellent guidepost for our ethos and aims.

In partnership with InterVarsity Press, we are pleased to offer a line of resources authored by a diverse range of theological practitioners. The resources in this series are selected based on the important way in which they address and embody these values, and thus, the unique contribution they offer in equipping Christian leaders for fuller and more faithful participation in God's mission.

Available Titles

The Church as Movement by JR Woodward and Dan White Jr., 978-0-8308-4133-2

Emboldened by Tara Beth Leach, 978-0-8308-4524-8

Embrace by Leroy Barber, 978-0-8308-4471-5

Faithful Presence by David E. Fitch, 978-0-8308-4127-1

God Is Stranger by Krish Kandiah, 978-0-8308-4532-3

Paradoxology by Krish Kandiah, 978-0-8308-4504-0

Redeeming Sex by Debra Hirsch, 978-0-8308-3639-0

Rediscipling the White Church by David W. Swanson, 978-0-8308-4597-2

Seven Practices for the Church on Mission by David E. Fitch, 978-0-8308-4142-4

A Sojourner's Truth by Natasha Sistrunk Robinson, 978-0-8308-4552-1

What Does It Mean to Be Welcoming? by Travis Collins, 978-0-8308-4144-8

White Awake by Daniel Hill, 978-0-8308-4393-0

missioalliance.org | twitter.com/missioalliance | facebook.com/missioalliance